ASTERISK BOOKS™

EXCELLENT RESULTS

EDEXCEL

ECONOMICS A REVISION GUIDE

FOR A-LEVEL YEAR 1 AND AS

BY KEVIN LONGE

First published in 2016 by Asterisk Books

Copyright © 2016 Kevin Longe

ISBN 978-0-9955584-1-0

Cover photo/illustration © art4all/Shutterstock.com

SECTION 1 – MICROECONOMICS

Scarcity and Choice

How Competitive Markets Work

Market Failure and Government Intervention

SECTION 2 – MACROECONOMICS

Macroeconomic Indicators and Economic Policy Objectives

Aggregate Demand and Aggregate Supply

The Global Context

TABLE OF CONTENTS

ECONOMICS A

ASTERISK BOOKS™

EXCELLENT RESULTS

 www.asteriskbooks.co.uk

WEBSITE

Check out our website for new book releases and free online resources (e.g. essays) that complement this book!

 asteriskbookscontact@gmail.com

 Asterisk Books

CONTACT US

If you have any concerns, need any help, or simply want to request that an essay (or any other material) be added to our website, feel free to contact us via email or The Student Room.

SECTION 1
MICROECONOMICS

1.1 THE FUNDAMENTALS OF ECONOMICS

Economics – The study of how to most effectively allocate scarce resources

Microeconomics – The study of individual economic agents and their decision making

Scarcity – A situation where there are insufficient resources to meet people's unlimited wants

Sustainability – Using resources so as not to compromise future generations' standard or quality of life

Goods – Tangible products that can be touched and measured e.g. cars, food, washing machines

Services – Intangible products that cannot be touched or measured e.g. banking, insurance, healthcare NOTE – For example, you can't measure the effort someone has put into healthcare

Utility – The total satisfaction received from consuming a good or service

Needs – Goods or services that are required to maintain existence / life e.g. food, water, shelter

Wants – Goods or services that we desire but are not necessary for maintaining existence / life e.g. cars, watches, TVs

Renewable Resources – Natural resources of economic value that can be replaced or replenished, or simply aren't used up e.g. wood, solar energy, wind energy

Non-Renewable Resources – Natural resources of economic value that cannot be readily replaced by natural means on a level equivalent to their consumption e.g. oil, natural gas, coal

Positive Statements – Statements that do not have to be correct, but must be able to be tested, and proved or disproved e.g. the UK's annual GDP growth rate was 2% in January 2016 NOTE – Positive statements can be proven or disproven by simply examining data

Normative Statements – Statements that are opinion based and so cannot be proved or disproved e.g. the government should provide basic education to all citizens NOTE – The previous example cannot be proved or disproved. It is not possible to prove that the government 'should' do anything, it's value based. On top of that, what constitutes 'basic' education? It's subjective

The Basic Economic Problem:

- The basic economic problem is essentially that **there are unlimited wants but scarce / limited resources, resulting in choices having to be made by households, firms and governments** (a problem that is experienced by every country in existence)
- The goal of economics is to find out **how best to allocate scarce resources among alternative uses,** in order to maximise the net utility (satisfaction) of societies (in the short run and long run)
- The **three main objectives of economics (WHW)** are essentially to decide:
  - **What** goods and services to produce
  - **How** to produce these goods and services
  - **Whom** to produce these goods and services for

1.2 OPPORTUNITY COST AND ECONOMIC AGENTS

Opportunity Cost – The potential value of the next best alternative, which is forgone when a choice is made

Economic Goods – Goods that impose some cost on society when produced. They are scarce / limited, and so have opportunity cost e.g. TVs, cars, chairs etc… NOTE – If you pay £0 for a packet of crisps, that does not make it a free good. There would still be a cost to society in terms of the limited resources used to make the plastic, the limited farmland used to plant the potatoes etc…

Free Goods – Goods that impose no cost on society when produced. They are unlimited, and so have no opportunity cost e.g. air, sunlight etc… NOTE – These goods tend to be ones that are produced by nature, with no need for any human and/or capital aid to the production process. This is unlike, for example, paper or tables which require trees to be cut down by humans (physical labour cost) and processing in a factory (physical labour cost of creating and then using the capital in the factory)

Opportunity Cost:

- Opportunity cost could essentially be said to be the benefit one could have received by taking an alternative action
- For example, the opportunity cost of going to university is the money you could have earned if you went straight into work instead NOTE – People tend to go to university in the hope that their degree will earn them more money during their career, and so hopefully result in them making up for the lost wages / salaries they sacrificed whilst in university
- What constitutes the 'next best alternative' depends on monetary value (e.g. choosing to get a £45,000 salaried job, rather than a £35,000 salaried job), value judgements (e.g. living close to home or being geographically mobile) or both in some cases
- In short, opportunity cost is the risk that you could have achieved greater benefits (be they monetary, time related, utility related etc…) with an alternative choice
- NOTE – In reality, people don't really have the time / can't be bothered to calculate the opportunity cost of their decisions. In many cases people can act irrationally, not caring about the opportunity cost, even if they can calculate the opportunity cost (roughly or accurately). Opportunity cost, however, is still a useful tool for evaluating the decisions of economic agents

Economic Agents – Decision makers that have effects on the economy of a country by buying, producing, selling, investing, taxing etc… NOTE – The three types of economic agents are households, firms and governments

Economic Agents:

- **Household –** A group of consumers that buy goods and services. They also supply their labour to firms to produce goods and services, in order to earn the income needed to purchase goods and services
- **Firm –** An organisation that uses factors of production alongside each other in order to produce output. They produce goods and services demanded by consumers

- **Government** – A governing body / organisation that undertakes expenditure (spending) and impacts the economy via taxation and the regulation of markets

1.3 FACTORS OF PRODUCTION AND PRODUCTION POSSIBILITY CURVES (PPCS)

Factors of Production – The available resource inputs used in the production process of goods and services

Factors of Production (CELL) – Capital + Entrepreneurship + Labour + Land

Factors of Production:

- **Capital** – Man-made aids for production; goods used to make other goods e.g. MERC – Machines + Equipment + Robots + Computers
- **Entrepreneurship** – The willingness of an entrepreneur to take risks and organise production NOTE – An entrepreneur is someone who bears the risks of a business and organises production
- **Labour** – The human resource that is available in an economy; the quantity and quality of human resources
- **Land** – The natural resource that is available in an economy; the quantity and quality of natural resources e.g. oil, coal, rivers, the land itself etc... NOTE – Some are renewable (e.g. trees, wind power etc...) and some non-renewable (e.g. coal, oil etc...)

Factors of Production (Factor Payments / Rewards / Incomes):

- The factors of production receive factor payments (rewards) for the services they provide. The corresponding rewards are as follows:
  - Capital receives rewards in the form of **interest**
  - Entrepreneurs receive rewards in the form of **profits**
  - Labour receives rewards in the form of **wages** (or salaries)
  - Land receives rewards in the form of **rent**

Consumer Goods – Goods bought and used by consumers for present use; final goods used for consumption means rather than production ones e.g. food, TVs, cars, watches etc...

Model – A simplified representation of reality used to create hypotheses (or theories) about economic decisions and events NOTE – Models tend to have a large number of assumptions that are then removed slowly. This is so that the change in outcome, resulting from the removal of each assumption, can be analysed. Models do not have to be 100% realistic as simplifying the real world is too complex, however, they should be accurate enough to allow sensible predictions to be made

Production Possibility Curve (PPC) – A curve showing the maximum quantities of different combinations of goods and/or services that can be produced in a set time period, given available resources and the current state of technology **NOTE – These can also be called production possibility frontiers (PPFs) or possibility transformation curves (PTCs)**

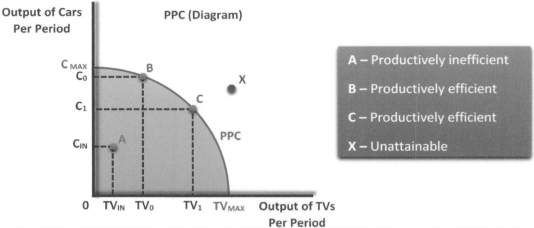

A – Productively inefficient

B – Productively efficient

C – Productively efficient

X – Unattainable

The curved green line is known as the PPC and essentially shows the maximum level of production of two products, given the limited resources available and current state of technology. Let's assume that this is an economy that only produces TVs and cars. If the economy decides to produce only cars, they can produce C_{MAX} number of cars and 0 TVs, and if they decide to produce only TVs, they can produce TV_{MAX} number of TVs and 0 cars. You can see that the PPC above is a curve rather than a straight line. This is because cars and TVs are imperfect substitutes.

When the economy moves towards total specialisation in one good, TVs, for example, it becomes increasingly difficult to produce the other good (cars) as the factors of production are not equally suited for production of both goods. This means that the few workers left to produce cars will have little resources left to work with, and so will struggle to greater and greater extents as the economy specialises more towards one good (TVs in this example, but it goes both ways) – this is known as the law of increasing opportunity cost. This isn't the case with point A, as point A is a productively inefficient point, meaning that it is possible to increase output of both goods. This is also not the case with point X (which is unattainable), as there simply isn't enough resources in the economy to produce such levels of output. Point B, on the other hand, is productively efficient as all resources are being utilised, represented by output of C_0 and TV_0. When moving to point C, however, whilst it is still a productively efficient point, it results in the output of TVs increasing from TV_0 to TV_1, with the output of cars decreasing from C_0 to C_1. This shows a trade-off being made between the two goods. This trade-off will get increasingly costly due to the law of increasing opportunity cost, meaning that more and more cars will need to be sacrificed for the production of a single TV.

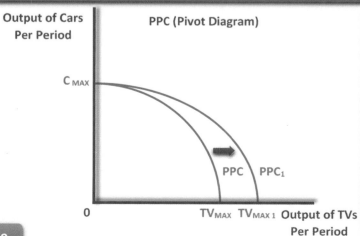

The diagram on the left shows another specific scenario, using the same examples. If a new innovation led to an improvement in the efficiency of the production process of TVs (specifically), whilst having no effect on the production process of cars, the PPC would pivot around C_{MAX} to create PPC_1. This would mean that a higher amount of TVs ($TV_{MAX\ 1}$, rather than just TV_{MAX} amount) could be created when the output of cars is 0. If the production process innovation was in the car industry instead, this would simply result in the PPC pivoting around TV_{MAX} instead.

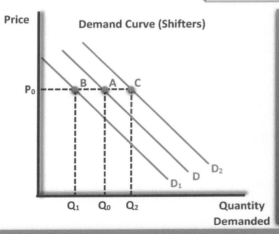

Demand Curve (Shifters)

Whilst we have looked at price changes and what they do to the quantity demanded of a product, it is also important to look at non-price factors and how they can have an effect on the quantity demanded of a product. If there is say, a decrease in average incomes, possibly due to a recession (resulting in a lot of people being out of jobs), then it is possible that without any change in price, the total amount of people willing and able to purchase a given product (e.g. a can of coke) may decrease, resulting in demand decreasing (shifting to the left) from D to D_1. This results in the same price of the product (P_0) resulting in a lower quantity demanded of the product (Q_1 rather than Q_0), simply due to the fall in overall demand.

Conversely, if, for example, Coca Cola increased advertising of its products, then it is possible that the total amount of people willing and able to purchase the product (a Coca Cola can, in this case) would increase, simply due to the increased awareness. This is because some people who may have been happy to buy a Coca Cola can may not have (simply due to not knowing about its existence), and those who already knew about it may have been reminded of how much they like it. As a consequence, the increase in demand (shift to the right) from D to D_2, can result in the same price of the product (P_0) leading to a higher quantity demanded of the product (Q_2 rather than Q_0), simply due to the increase in overall demand. There are several non-price factors which have these effects (these will be listed below).

PRIEST ALI (Demand Shifters / Determinants / Conditions):

P – Population – If there is a change in the size of the population, this will change the total amount of people willing and able to buy any given product, thus changing demand **e.g. increase in population size (e.g. due to increased immigration) → increase in demand for any given product**

R – Related Goods – If there is a change in the price of a substitute for a product, or a change in the price of a complement for a product, this will lead to a change in demand for said product **e.g. increase in the price of a substitute product (e.g. Pepsi cans) → increase in demand for Coca Cola cans NOTE – This is actually related to what is known as 'cross elasticity of demand (XED)'. This will be discussed in much greater detail, later in this chapter**

I – Interest Rates – If there is a change in interest rates, this will change the cost of borrowing and the amount of money received in return for those who save. This will change the total amount of people willing and able to buy any given product, and so change demand as well **e.g. decrease in interest rates → cheaper to borrow, less return from savings → increase in total spending → increase in demand for any given product NOTE – Interest rates will be discussed in far greater detail in chapter 5.1**

E – Expectations of Future Prices – If there is a change in the expectation of the future price of a product, this will lead to a change in the current level of demand for said specific product **e.g. price of oil is expected to increase in the future → increase in demand for oil now**

S – Seasons – If there is a change in seasons, this is likely to lead to a change in demand for a given set of products **e.g. winter is coming → increase in demand for winter jackets and coats, and a decrease in demand for thin t-shirts and shorts (other products may be affected as well)**

T – Tastes – If there is a change in the tastes of consumers, such as a new fashion trend or a rising social trend towards higher living standards (e.g. people wanting virtual reality products), this will lead to a change in demand e.g. increasing fashion trend for jeggings → increase in demand for jeggings

A – Advertising – If there is a change in the level of advertising for a product (e.g. Coca Cola cans) this will likely lead to a change in demand for said specific product (due to increased awareness) e.g. increase in advertising for Coca Cola cans → increase in demand for Coca Cola cans

L – Legislation – For example, if a motorcycle helmet law is introduced, requiring that everyone must wear a helmet on a motorcycle, this would lead to an increase in demand for motorcycle helmets

I – Average Disposable Income – If there is a change in the level of average disposable income, this will change the total amount of people willing and able to buy any given product, thus changing demand e.g. average disposable income rises → rise in demand for any given product **NOTE – Disposable income is essentially people's level of income after taxes have been deducted and state benefits have been added. This concept hasn't been discussed yet, but will be in chapter 5.1. Also, bear in mind that the effects of average disposable income on demand depend on the YED of the product (YED will be discussed later in this chapter)**

Veblen / Snob Good – A good for which the quantity demanded increases as the price increases, because of its exclusive nature and allure as a status symbol e.g. designer, luxury items with a strong brand identity such as a Rolex watch NOTE – It leads to an upwards sloping demand curve, contrary to the law of demand. It is a special case

Price

Demand Curve (Veblen Good)

D

Quantity Demanded

Veblen / snob goods are thought to lead to what is known as 'conspicuous consumption'. This is because, unlike a typical good, the quantity demanded for a Veblen good increases as its price increases because consumers see it as an exclusive status symbol, resulting in an upwards sloping demand curve. The goods are expensive so that only the very affluent can afford them; the higher their price, the less likely other consumers can afford them, and the more buyers perceive them to signal great wealth and success. If a Veblen good's price decreases, demand will decrease because status conscious consumers will see it as less exclusive (e.g. Michael Kors bags).

Elasticity – A measure of a variable's sensitivity relative to a change in another variable

Price Elasticity of Demand (PED) – A measure of the responsiveness of quantity demanded relative to a change in the price of a good or service

Price Elasticity of Demand (PED) Formula(s) – $\dfrac{\%\ change\ in\ quantity\ demanded}{\%\ change\ in\ price}$ OR $\dfrac{Original\ Price}{Original\ Quantity\ Demanded} \times \dfrac{numerical\ change\ in\ quantity\ demanded}{numerical\ change\ in\ price}$

Price Inelastic Demand – Where the percentage change in the quantity demanded of a product is insensitive to a change in the price of the product ($0 < |PED| < 1$) e.g. if the price of Starbucks coffee increased, there would be a fall in the amount of units (of coffee) they sold, but it would likely be a very small one due to the brand loyalty and addiction many of us have to companies like Starbucks and their products

Price Elastic Demand – Where the percentage change in the quantity demanded of a product is sensitive to a change in the price of the product ($|PED| > 1$) e.g. if the price of Walkers crisps increased, you may feel inclined to buy a lot less as there are a lot of other substitutes in the form of other crisp packet brands and also in the form of other snacks (e.g. peanuts, biscuits)

Price Unitary Elastic Demand – Where the percentage change in the quantity demanded of a product is equal to a change in the price of the product ($|PED| = 1$)

NOTE – The '$|\ |$' symbols mean 'absolute value' which essentially means the 'positive value'. The reason these symbols are used will make sense shortly

Percentage Change Formula – $\frac{New\ Figure - Old\ Figure}{Old\ Figure} \times 100$

PED Conditions:

- **Perfectly Price Inelastic Demand:** $|PED| = 0$
- **Relatively Price Inelastic Demand:** $0 < |PED| < 1$
- **Price Unitary Elastic Demand:** $|PED| = 1$
- **Relatively Price Elastic Demand:** $1 < |PED| < \infty$
- **Perfectly Price Elastic Demand:** $|PED| = \infty$

PED Numeric Example:

- Taking an iPhone 6s, for example, let's imagine that the price of an iPhone 6s rose from £540 to £594, resulting in the quantity demanded of the iPhone 6s falling from 10,000 units to 9,500 units
- Plugging in the change in quantity demanded of the product into the percentage change formula, results in $\frac{9,500 - 10,000}{10,000} \times 100 = -5\%$
- Plugging in the price change into the percentage change formula, results in $\frac{594 - 540}{540} \times 100 = 10\%$
- Plugging these into the first PED formula gives us $-\frac{5}{10} = -0.5$
- This negative value explains why we use the absolute (positive) value when interpreting PED. Technically speaking you could just use the negative values and interpret them as they are, but most people find it confusing to do so and so, for the sake of simplicity, just use the positive version **NOTE –** Always remember, however, that the initial value you get from a PED calculation should always be negative
- The negative value makes sense as the demand curve is downwards sloping, and so if price increases, quantity demanded will fall, and if price falls, quantity demanded will rise, meaning that there will always be a negative and a positive in the (percentage change) fraction, resulting in a negative PED value
- Interpreting this PED value leads to the conclusion that the PED for iPhone 6s's is relatively inelastic, or you could say that the demand for iPhone 6s's is relatively price inelastic. This is because $|-0.5| = 0.5$ and $0.5 < 1$, which meets the inelastic PED condition ($0 < |PED| < 1$)

- This tells us that consumers of iPhone 6s's are insensitive to changes in the price of the product, and so their changes in demand (specifically, quantity demanded) of the product will change by an amount that is small relative to the price change NOTE – This would be expected due to the brand loyalty that many consumers have for apple products. The factors affecting price elasticity of demand will be discussed shortly
- If we had instead got, for example, a figure of -1.5, we would consider PED to be relatively elastic (or demand to be relatively price elastic) as $|-1.5| = 1.5$, and $1.5 > 1$. Using a 10% price fall, for example, would tell us that a 10% fall in the price of this product (with -1.5 PED) would lead to a 15% rise in quantity demanded for said product
- Examples could of course be done to show a unit (or unitary) elastic PED outcome, but I think with these numeric examples you should be well equipped enough to answer any such questions
- NOTE – The perfectly price inelastic and perfectly price elastic conditions will be discussed briefly later, however, bear in mind that they are just theoretical ideas and not likely to be seen with any product in the real world

HITS BND (PED Determinants):

H – **Habit-Forming Goods** – Habit-forming goods (or addictive goods) tend to have very price inelastic demand. This is because those who consume them become somewhat dependent on them for utility (satisfaction) in their lives, and so price rises, for example, do little to affect their consumption e.g. cigarettes

I – **Proportion of Income** – Goods that take up a larger proportion of income tend to have more price elastic demand. This is because changes in the prices of such products have a greater effect on the incomes of those who purchase them (they more heavily reduce, or increase, the ability of those consumers to buy other products) e.g. a TV

T – **Time Period (Short Run / Long Run)** – Consumers are less likely to change spending habits in the short run, however, in the long run they may become more aware of substitutes which increases price elasticity of demand (makes PED more elastic)

S – **The Availability and Closeness of Substitutes** – The higher the amount of substitutes available for a product, and the more closely related these substitutes are (the smaller the difference between the product and its substitutes), the more price elastic demand is likely to be e.g. biscuits (price elastic demand), or on the opposite end, petrol (not many close substitutes, so it has very price inelastic demand)

B – **Brand Loyalty** – Products with strong brands tend to have more price inelastic demand. This is because the loyalty consumers have to the product can make them care less about price changes, simply due to their trust in the company or some particular liking they have towards the company e.g. Apple and Starbucks products

N – **Necessities** – Goods that are necessities tend to have very price inelastic demands. This is because without them, serving the basic functions of life would most likely be a struggle, and so even if its price rises, it will not affect your consumption greatly as you essentially need it (to some reasonable extent) for survival e.g. milk, water, bread etc...

D – Durability – Goods that are expected to last a long time tend to have more price elastic demand as the purchase can be delayed, whereas a product like milk will run out quickly and need to be repurchased even if its price rises **e.g. a table (more price elastic demand)**

NOTE – Some of these points may seem slightly contradictory in the sense that some products fall under several determinants in opposing directions, however, the idea is that each product has certain push factors that ultimately determine whether or not the product is more LIKELY to have price elastic or price inelastic demand

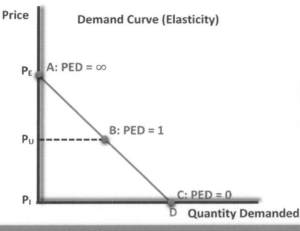

The diagram on the left shows that PED changes along any demand curve that is a straight line. If we, for a moment, use the second PED formula:

$$\frac{Original\ Price}{Original\ Quantity\ Demanded} \times \frac{change\ in\ quantity\ demanded}{change\ in\ price}$$

we will be able to show why this is true.

When the price is P_E we can notice that the quantity demanded is 0, resulting in 'Original Quantity Demanded' in the formula being 0. You may not know this if you don't do Maths A-Level, but if we have a 0 on the bottom of a fraction, that results in an undefined answer, specifically, infinity in this case (the condition for perfectly price elastic demand), and so PED = ∞ at A. If we now move to P_I we can see that price (P_I) at this point is 0, and so 'Original Price' in the formula is 0. Once again, you may only know this if you do Maths A-Level, but a 0 on top of a fraction results in a final answer of 0 (the condition for perfectly price inelastic demand), and so PED = 0. From this we can deduce that the midpoint of the straight line will have a point where PED = 1 (the condition for unitary price elastic demand), and so we can see that PED does indeed change across a straight line. This effect occurs because when price is relatively high, the initial quantity is very low. This means that a small change in price from a high price will result in a relatively small percentage change in price, whereas the small change in quantity would result in a relatively large percentage change as the initial quantity would be very small. The opposite is true at the bottom of the demand curve.

Total Revenue (TR) – The total amount of money received for goods sold or services provided over a certain time period

Total Revenue (TR) Formula – $Price \times Quantity$

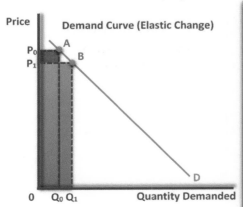

The diagram on the left shows the effects of elasticity on TR. As the demand curve is price elastic in the top half, we can see the effects of a price drop and its effect on TR. A price drop from P_0 to P_1, results in quantity demanded increasing from Q_0 to Q_1. As the formula for TR is $Price \times Quantity$, the change in TR is well shown by the coloured boxes. The initial TR is P_0AQ_00, then changing to P_1BQ_10. The lost TR is shown by the red rectangle, and the gained TR is shown by the green rectangle. From this, it is clear to see that a fall in price along the elastic part of the curve, results in an increase in TR, as the gain (the green rectangle) is greater than what is lost (the red rectangle), and so, overall, TR has increased. The opposite is of course also true, and so if you increase the price on the elastic part of the curve, TR will decrease.

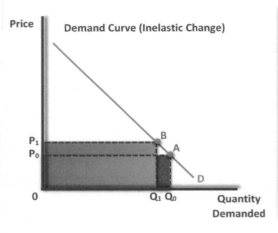

Demand Curve (Inelastic Change)

As the demand curve is price inelastic in the bottom half, we can see the effects of a price rise and its effect on TR. A price rise from P_0 to P_1, results in quantity demanded decreasing from Q_0 to Q_1. The initial TR is P_0AQ_00, then changing to P_1BQ_10. Once again, the lost TR is shown by the red rectangle, and the gained TR is shown by the green rectangle. From this, it is clear to see that a rise in price along the inelastic part of the curve, results in an increase in TR, as the gain (the green rectangle) is greater than what is lost (the red rectangle), and so, overall, TR has increased. The opposite is of course also true, and so if you decrease the price on the inelastic part of the curve TR will decrease.

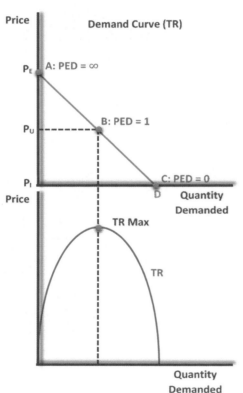

The diagram on the left finalises the idea of the demand curve and TR. Following the logic from the two previous graphs, it essentially shows us that along the price elastic part of the demand curve (between A and B) we should decrease the price until we reach unit elasticity at price P_U (regardless of whether the start price was P_E or in between P_E and P_U). The graph also shows that along the price inelastic part of the demand curve (between C and B) we should increase the price until we reach unit elasticity at price P_U (regardless of whether the start price was P_I or in between P_I and P_U). Through this, a firm can maximise their TR.

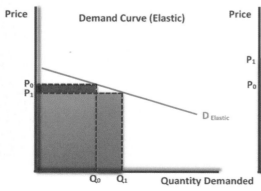

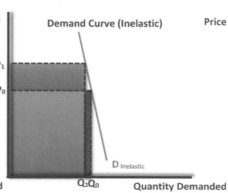

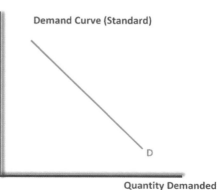

Now (looking at the graphs on the previous page) you may be wondering 'Why has the demand curve suddenly changed slope to represent a price elastic or price inelastic demand curve?'. You may or may not have already realised this, but this is to do with where the midpoint of each curve is. The fact that the diagram on the left is drawn as a very shallow curve means that the midpoint of the curve (the part where it becomes unit elastic) is way off onto the far bottom right of the graph. This basically ensures that if you want to show that something has price elastic demand, the TR values, price, and quantity demanded changes, will make sense, because across the part of the curve made visible $|PED| > 1$. For the graph in the middle, the demand curve is drawn as a very steep curve because that means that the midpoint of the curve (the part where it becomes unit elastic) is way off in the top left of the graph. This ensures that if you want to instead show that something has price inelastic demand, the TR values, price, and quantity demanded changes, will make sense, because across the part of the curve made visible $0 < |PED| < 1$. You could basically say, it's almost as if you are zooming in on a desired part of the previous demand curve graph, and changing the slope so that you can deal only with what you want. When in an exam, if you are asked to talk about high or low elasticity (price elastic or price inelastic demand), you will want to draw the demand curve the same way as in the graphs (on the previous page) to make your point.

Just to ensure that you truly understand this for yourself and are not just taking my word for it, you can see the effects of a price change on both curves. On the price elastic demand curve, you can see that the change (fall in this case) in price from P_0 to P_1, is small relative to the change (increase in this case) in quantity demanded from Q_0 to Q_1, hence showing that quantity demanded is very sensitive relative to changes in price. Having explained the idea of how TR is shown using the coloured boxes, I won't explain it again, so assuming you read the earlier parts it should be clear visually to you that the effects on TR are the same as what was shown before on the old demand curve (increase in TR when the price falls on the price elastic demand curve). Conversely, on the price inelastic demand curve, you can see that the change (rise in this case) in price from P_0 to P_1, is large relative to the change (fall in this case) of quantity demanded from Q_0 to Q_1, hence showing that quantity demanded is not very sensitive relative to changes in price. Once again, assuming you read the earlier parts, it should be clear visually to you that the effects on TR are the same as what was shown before on the old demand curve (increase in TR when the price rises on the price inelastic demand curve). If, in a question, the curve you need to draw doesn't need to be specifically elastic or inelastic, then just draw the standard demand curve (on the right). The standard demand curve, just like all others, will have elasticity change along it, but unlike the other two, it is not drawn in such a way that it is trying to show only elastic or only inelastic changes.

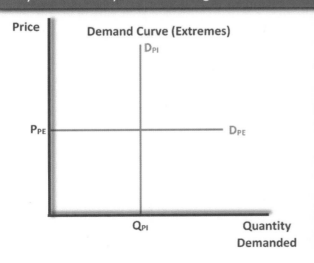

The diagram on the left shows some extreme (mostly theoretical) cases of PED. If $|PED| = 0$ that would result in perfectly price inelastic demand (D_{PI}). This would mean that the quantity demanded of the product would be completely insensitive to changes in price, and so the quantity demanded would be fixed at Q_{PI}. If instead $|PED| = \infty$, that would result in perfectly price elastic demand (D_{PE}). This would mean that the quantity demanded of the product would be an infinite amount (unlimited quantity) at the price P_{PE}. Firms would have no incentive to lower price below this level, but if they were to raise price above P_{PE}, quantity demanded would fall to 0.

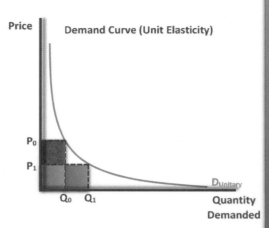

Price

Demand Curve (Unit Elasticity)

P_0

P_1

$D_{Unitary}$

Q_0 Q_1

Quantity Demanded

Now, if you're looking at this thinking that it makes no sense, it's understandable, as this isn't likely to make intuitive sense. The idea is that if $|PED| = 1$, resulting in a unitary price elastic demand curve ($D_{Unitary}$), then any percentage change in price should be offset by an equal and opposite percentage change in quantity demanded. This can be seen reasonably well with the change (fall) in price from P_0 to P_1 being identical in size to the change (increase) in quantity demanded from Q_0 to Q_1. This results in there being no change in TR, as the lost TR is the same size as the gained TR. If you get asked to identify a truly unitary price elastic demand curve, in an exam, you know what it technically should look like. It is very unlikely, however, that they would ever ask such a question. When answering a question, if they don't specify elasticity, unless you know that demand should be price elastic or inelastic (e.g. demand for cigarettes should be price inelastic), just use the standard demand curve.

Income Elasticity of Demand (YED) – A measure of the responsiveness of quantity demanded relative to a change in income

Income Elasticity of Demand (YED) Formula – $\frac{\% \text{ change in quantity demanded}}{\% \text{ change in income}}$

Relatively Income Inelastic Demand – Goods for which a change in income produces a less than proportionate change in quantity demanded $(0 < |YED| < 1)$

Relatively Income Elastic Demand – Goods for which a change in income produces a greater than proportionate change in quantity demanded $(1 < |YED| < \infty)$

Income Unitary Elastic Demand – Goods for which a change in income produces a proportionate change in quantity demanded $(|YED| = 1)$

Percentage Change Formula – $\frac{New \ Figure - Old \ Figure}{Old \ Figure} \times 100$

Normal Good – A good where the quantity demanded increases when income rises $(YED > 0)$
NOTE – There are two types of normal goods: superior (luxury) goods and necessity goods

Superior (Luxury) Good – A good where the quantity demanded increases by a proportionately greater amount than a rise in income $(YED > 1)$ e.g. iPhones (you are likely to buy a lot more if your income rises)

Necessity Good – A good where the quantity demanded increases by a proportionately smaller amount than a rise in income $(0 < YED < 1)$ e.g. bread (if your income rose you probably wouldn't spend that much more money on bread)

Inferior Good – A good where the quantity demanded decreases when income rises $(YED < 0)$ e.g. bus travel (if your income rises, you are more likely to spend less on bus travel and just travel by taxi or a personal car instead)

Giffen Good – A good where the quantity demanded decreases by a proportionately greater amount than a rise in income $(YED < -1)$ e.g. YED = -2: income rises by 10% → quantity demanded for good (Giffen good) falling by 20% NOTE – This is a special case (it's an extreme type of an inferior good) and will be discussed shortly

YED Numeric Example:

- Taking an iPhone 6s as an example, let's imagine that average income rose from £20,000 to £22,000, resulting in the quantity demanded of the iPhone 6s increasing from 10,000 units to 12,000 units

- Plugging in the change in quantity demanded of the product into the percentage change formula, results in $\frac{12,000-10,000}{10,000} \times 100 = 20\%$

- Plugging in the average income change into the percentage change formula, results in $\frac{22,000-20,000}{20,000} \times 100 = 10\%$

- Plugging these into the YED formula gives us $\frac{20}{10} = +2$

- The fact that the YED value is positive tells us that this must be a normal good, a good whose quantity demanded increases when income rises

- The fact that YED is not only positive (YED > 0) but is indeed greater than 1 (YED = 2, and 2 >1) means that this is indeed a superior (luxury) good, one whose quantity demanded increases by an amount that is proportionally larger than the rise in income (20% change in quantity demanded > 10% change in average income)

- This is what we would expect with iPhones because it would be considered a luxury good, in society, that people would consume much more of (buying it more often, or more in one go) if they had more income

- If we instead got, for example, a figure of – 0.5 for the YED value, this would be considered an inferior good. This would mean that quantity demanded for such a product would actually fall as average income rose (i.e. people would consume less of it). For example, if average income rose by 10%, quantity demanded, for such a product, would fall by 5%. This would be representative of a product such as bus travel (you would prefer to travel by taxi or a personal car) or tinned meat (you would rather eat fresh meat), whereby you would decrease your spending on such items if your income rose

- Examples could be done to show a unit (or unitary) elastic or positive relatively income inelastic (necessity good) YED outcome, but I think that with these numeric examples you should be well equipped enough to answer any such questions NOTE – I don't believe that there is a specific name for a good with a YED of 1, apart from it just being a normal good

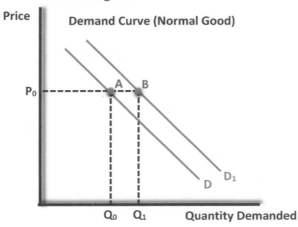

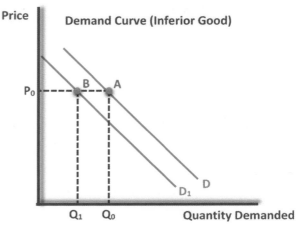

The graphs on the previous page show the different effects of a rise in average disposable income on different types of goods. For a normal good (left graph) a rise in average disposable income should lead to a rise in demand from D to D_1, resulting in quantity demanded increasing from Q_0 to Q_1 at the same price P_0. Whether or not the good is a necessity or a superior (luxury) good, demand will still increase, the only difference is that the superior (luxury) good's demand curve would increase by more than the necessity good's demand curve. For an inferior good (right graph) a rise in average disposable income should lead to a fall in demand from D to D_1, resulting in quantity demanded falling from Q_0 to Q_1 at the same price P_0. Keep this in mind in case Edexcel try to fool you in an exam.

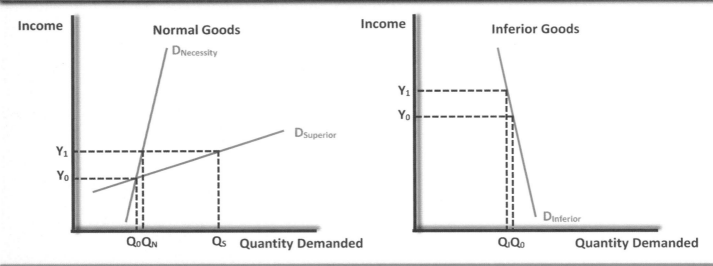

Now, before you start thinking 'Why are there two upwards sloping demand curves?', notice that the y-axis has changed from 'Price' to 'Income'. The diagram on the left shows how quantity demanded changes relative to income for the two types of normal goods: necessity goods and superior (luxury) goods. The demand for the necessity goods is income inelastic (shown by the $D_{Necessity}$ curve) and the demand for the superior (luxury) good is income elastic (shown by the $D_{Superior}$ curve). We can see from the graph that an equal rise in income from Y_0 to Y_1, leads to quantity demanded of the necessity increasing from Q_0 to Q_N, and quantity demanded for the superior good increasing from Q_0 to Q_S. This graph makes it clear that the quantity demanded for the necessity has risen by an amount less than proportionate to the rise in income ($Q_N - Q_0 < Y_1 - Y_0$), and the quantity demanded for the superior (luxury) good has risen by an amount greater than proportionate to the rise in income ($Q_S - Q_0 > Y_1 - Y_0$). The graph on the right shows the relationship between quantity demanded and income for an inferior good (shown by the $D_{Inferior}$ curve). It simply shows that a rise in income from Y_0 to Y_1, leads to a fall in quantity demanded from Q_0 to Q_I. This graph makes it clear that the quantity demanded for the inferior good has fallen by an amount less than proportionate to the change in income ($Q_0 - Q_I < Y_1 - Y_0$) as demand for most inferior goods is income inelastic.

NOTE – The concept of a Giffen good isn't explicitly mentioned in the specification, and so if you don't understand it, I wouldn't stress about it as it's highly unlikely to show up in an actual exam

Giffen Good Conditions:

- Must be an essential staple good in a poor community with few, if any, substitutes
- The households must be so poor that they only consume staple foods
- The good must be a very inferior good (YED < -1)

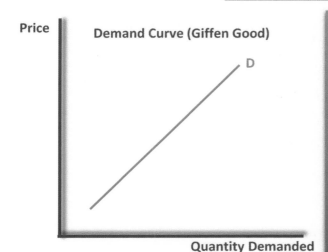

Price

Demand Curve (Giffen Good)

D

Quantity Demanded

A Giffen good is a special type of good that is considered to be mostly theoretical. The necessary conditions for a Giffen good result in this upwards sloping demand curve. We discussed earlier that the reasons for the demand curve being downwards sloping were largely due to the income and substitution effects. With a Giffen good, the substitution effect is heavily weakened due to the fact that as the price of the good rises, consumers can't switch to alternatives because they consider the good (the Giffen good) to be an essential staple food for which there are basically no other substitutes. Secondly, a rise in the price of this essential staple food will basically lead to a fall in average disposable income in the poor community, because that is basically what everyone spends almost all of their income on.

With inferior goods, whilst it is true that if income rises then quantity demanded for the inferior good will fall, it is also true that if income falls then quantity demanded for the inferior good will rise (it goes both ways). As stated previously, the rise in price has caused average disposable income to fall and so now (according to theory) quantity demanded for this inferior good (essential staple food) will rise. The resulting effect is this upwards sloping demand curve. Technically speaking, however, this effect will not continue forever due to the fact that at some point the poor consumers will simply have no more income to allocate to the product, and so likely run out of money. The only case in which such an effect is thought to have maybe occurred in real life was during the Irish potato famine in the 19th century, but even that claim is still disputable.

Substitutes – Products that can be used for a similar purpose, such that if the price of one product rises, demand for the other product is likely to rise **e.g. PS4 and Xbox One**

Complements – Products that tend to be consumed jointly, such that if the price of one product rises, demand for the other product is likely to fall **e.g. PS4 and PS4 video games, or tea and milk**

Competitive Demand – Demand for products that are competing with each other **NOTE – This type of demand is associated with substitutes**

Joint Demand – Demand for products which are interdependent, such that they are jointly demanded **NOTE – This type of demand is associated with complements**

Cross Elasticity of Demand (XED) – A measure of the responsiveness of quantity demanded for one product relative to a change in the price of another product

Cross Elasticity of Demand (XED) Formula – $\dfrac{\% \; change \; in \; quantity \; demanded \; of \; product \; X}{\% \; change \; in \; price \; of \; product \; Y}$

Percentage Change Formula – $\dfrac{New \; Figure - Old \; Figure}{Old \; Figure} \times 100$

Substitutes (XED Terminology) – Products which have a positive XED value **NOTE – A little trick (for any of you who play PS4) to remember is: PS+ = Positive Substitute**

Complements (XED Terminology) – Products which have a negative XED value **NOTE – A little trick to remember is: CNN = Complement Negative Number**

XED Conditions:

- **Two Products Have No Relation in Terms of Price Affecting Demand:** XED = 0
- **Substitutes:** XED > 0 (positive XED value)
- **Complements:** XED < 0 (negative XED value)
- **Weak Substitutes:** 0 < XED < 1 (positive XED, but in between 0 and 1)
- **Close Substitutes:** XED > 1 (positive XED and greater than 1)
- **Weak Complements:** -1 < XED < 0 (negative XED, but in between -1 and 0)
- **Close Complements:** XED < -1 (negative XED and less than -1)
- **Identical Products (Perfect Substitutes):** XED = ∞ e.g. currency (a unit of a currency, such as a $, from one foreign exchange market is exactly the same as one from another foreign exchange market)
- **One Good Must Be Bought Alongside the Other (Perfect Complements):** XED = $-\infty$ e.g. a left shoe and a right shoe (although they are always sold in pairs in the real world)

XED Numeric Example:

- Taking Xbox Ones and PS4s as examples, let's imagine that the price of Xbox Ones rose from £250 to £275, and the quantity demanded of PS4s rose from 10,000 units to 12,000 units
- Plugging in the change in quantity demanded of PS4s into the percentage change formula, results in $\frac{12,000-10,000}{10,000} \times 100 = 20\%$
- Plugging in the price change of Xbox Ones into the percentage change formula, results in $\frac{275-250}{250} \times 100 = 10\%$
- Plugging these into the YED formula gives us $\frac{20}{10} = +2$
- The fact that the XED value is positive tells us that these two goods must be substitutes, goods with competitive demand
- The fact that XED is not only positive (XED > 0) but is indeed greater than 1 (XED = 2, and 2 >1) means that these products are indeed close substitutes, goods with a very strong competitive demand (a 10% change in the price of Xbox Ones caused the amount of PS4's sold to increase by 20%, a clear indicator of the strength of their relationship)
- This is what we would expect for Xbox Ones and PS4s as they are both similar (in that they are both video game consoles) and they are both similarly priced, meaning that when one changes in price it is likely to affect the quantity demanded of the other strongly
- If we instead got, for example, a figure of – 2 for the XED value, these would be considered complementary goods. This would mean that quantity demanded for product X would fall if the price of good Y increased. For example, if the price of product Y rose by 10%, quantity demanded for product X would fall by 20%. This would be representative of PS4s and PS4 video games, for example, as a PS4's value is largely derived from the fact that you can play PS4 video games on it. If said PS4 video games, for example, increased in price, this may change your decision to buy a PS4 and thus result in a lower quantity demanded of PS4s overall
- Examples could of course be done to show weak substitutes, weak complements and products with no relationship, but I think that with these numeric examples, and the conditions above, you should be well equipped enough to answer any such questions

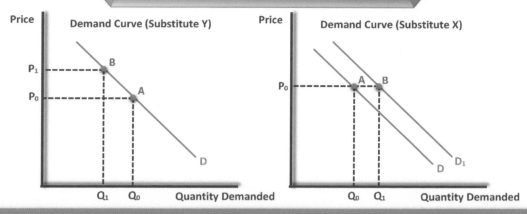

The above graphs simply show the potential effects of substitutes on each other. If the price of product Y increases from P_0 to P_1, and product Y and product X are substitutes, this will lead to demand for product X increasing from D to D_1, resulting in quantity demanded (for product X) increasing from Q_0 to Q_1 with price staying at P_0. The opposite effect would of course occur if the price of product Y fell, in which case demand for product X would fall.

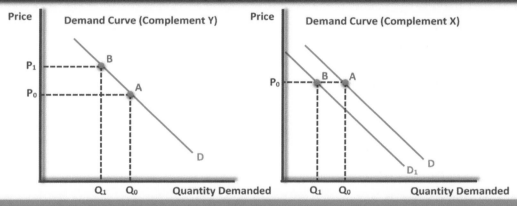

The above graphs simply show the potential effects of complements on each other. If the price of product Y increases from P_0 to P_1, and product Y and product X are complements, this will lead to demand for product X falling from D to D_1, resulting in quantity demanded (for product X) falling from Q_0 to Q_1 with price staying at P_0. The opposite effects would of course occur if the price of product Y fell, in which case demand for product X would rise.

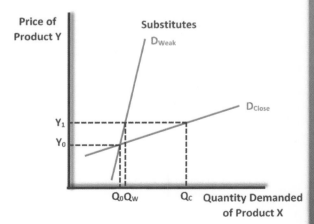

Now, before you start thinking 'Why are there two upwards sloping demand curves?', notice that the y-axis is 'Price of Product Y' and that the x-axis is 'Quantity Demanded of Product X'. The diagram on the left shows the difference between how the quantity demanded of product X changes relative to the price of product Y, depending on how weak or close (strong) the substitute relationship. The demand curve representing a weak substitute relationship is shown by the D_{Weak} curve, and the demand curve representing a close (strong) substitute relationship is shown by the D_{Close} curve. We can see from the graph that an equal rise in the price of product Y from Y_0 to Y_1, leads to quantity demanded of product X increasing from Q_0 to Q_W (when the relationship is weak) and from Q_0 to Q_C (when the relationship is close / strong). This graph makes it clear that the change in quantity demanded for product X is greater when the relationship between the goods is stronger.

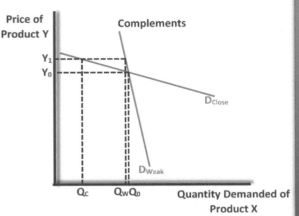

The diagram on the left shows the difference between how the quantity demanded of product X changes relative to the price of product Y, depending on how weak or close (strong) the complement relationship. The demand curve representing a weak complement relationship is shown by the D_{Weak} curve and the demand curve representing a close (strong) complement relationship is shown by the D_{Close} curve. We can see from the graph that an equal rise in the price of product Y from Y_0 to Y_1, leads to quantity demanded of product X decreasing from Q_0 to Q_W (when the relationship is weak) and from Q_0 to Q_C (when the relationship is close / strong). This graph, just like the previous one, makes it clear that the change in quantity demanded for product X is greater when the relationship between the goods is stronger.

NOTE – The following set of lists are rough guides as to how you may wish to answer questions on elasticities of demand. You would of course need to add in the specific detail needed to answer the question, and also add the context they are asking for, but generally these guidelines should help stop you from missing out key points

PED Question Response (Guidelines):

- Analysis:
- **PED Coefficient** – Elastic, Inelastic or Unit Elastic?
- **10% Example** – PED = -1.5 (for example): Price goes up by 10% → Quantity demanded falls by 15%
- Evaluation:
- **Does the PED value correspond with economic theory?** e.g. PED cannot be positive, or the PED for cigarettes should not be elastic
- PED values are **estimates and they may be unreliable**
- **Estimates can change over time**
- **Other factors can affect supply and demand**
- The analysis likely **assumes ceteris paribus, which may not apply** e.g. demand could shift left due to a fall in average disposable income

YED Question Response (Guidelines):

- Analysis:
- **YED Coefficient** – What type of good is it, and what is its elasticity?
- **10% Example** – YED = 1.5 (for example): Income goes up by 10% → Quantity demanded rises by 15%
- Evaluation:
- **Does the YED value correspond with economic theory?** e.g. A TV shouldn't be an inferior good
- **YED values are estimates and they may be unreliable**
- **Estimates can change over time**
- The analysis likely **assumes ceteris paribus which may not apply** e.g. if income tax has risen, this may mean that whilst there has been an increase in income, for example, disposable income may not have increased and so quantity demanded may not change

XED Question Response (Guidelines):

- Analysis:
- **XED Coefficient –** Are the goods substitutes or complements, and are they close or weak?
- **10% Example –** XED = 1.5 (for example): Price of product Y goes up by 10% → Quantity demanded of product X rises by 15%
- Evaluation:
- **Does the XED value correspond with economic theory?** e.g. PS4s and Xbox Ones are not complements, and so the XED value should be positive
- **XED values are estimates and they may be unreliable**
- **Estimates can change over time**
- **The analysis likely assumes ceteris paribus which may not apply** e.g. demand could shift left due to a fall in average disposable income

How Elasticity is Calculated in Reality:

- Elasticities of demand and supply (will be discussed shortly) are calculated, in reality, using the following data:
  - **Sample surveys**
  - **Past records from within a company**
  - **Competitor analysis**
- NOTE – This really highlights to you the unreliability of this information in real life, but the general theory of them is still useful to economic agents in some ways

Marginal Social Benefit (MSB) – The additional benefit that society gains from consuming one more unit of a product

Consumer Surplus – The extra amount of money that a consumer is willing to pay for a product above the price that they actually pay

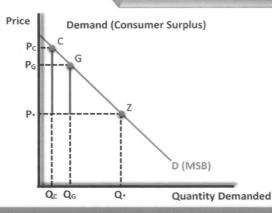

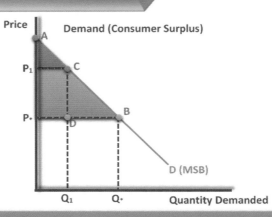

The demand curve represents more than just price and quantity demanded. Suppose that the price of a product was P_* with level of quantity demanded Q_*. P_* can effectively be looked at as the value that the last consumer (consumer Z) places on said product. Basically, if the price was even slightly above P_*, this last consumer (Z) would choose not to buy said product – this last consumer (Z) is known as the marginal consumer. To the marginal consumer, P_* represents the marginal (additional) benefit gained from consuming the product – in essence it is the price that reflects the individual consumer's (Z's) benefit from consuming the product, as it is the price that just induces them to purchase the product. If we move to looking at society as a whole (which includes all consumers), P_* can be said to be the MSB that is obtained from the consumption of said product. This applies at any point along the demand curve, and so any point on the demand curve can be interpreted as the MSB of consuming said product.

Whilst we can see that consumer Z paid the exact price they were willing to pay, it is true that in most markets everyone pays the same price, do they not? As a result, there are other consumers in the market paying this lower price of P_*, even though they are willing to pay more. Consumer C, for example, is willing to pay price P_C for this product for some unknown quantity (Q_C includes the units that consumer A and B are willing to buy, and so technically consumer C is willing to buy $Q_C - Q_B - Q_A$ units, but this isn't shown on the diagram), but this price is higher than the actual price of the product (P_*). As a result, consumer C is receiving a consumer surplus of size $P_C - P_*$, represented by the left vertical green line. Similarly, consumer G is also receiving a consumer surplus, in their case, one of size $P_G - P_*$, represented by the right vertical green line. If all of the surpluses (through A to Z) were added up, they would sum to create the total consumer surplus that society gains from consuming said product.

The total surplus is shown by the graph on the right. At a price of P_* and a quantity demanded of Q_*, the total consumer surplus is the triangle ABP_* (the letters have no reference to the consumers from before, so you can label them as anything you want), which is shown by the small green triangle plus the bigger grey right-angled trapezium. Effectively, this means that the space above the price, below the demand curve and to the right of the y-axis, can be regarded as the total consumer surplus. In addition to this, however, it is worth knowing that changes in price affect the size of the consumer surplus. If price increased from P_* to P_1, resulting in quantity demanded falling from Q_* to Q_1, this would lead to the consumer surplus decreasing from the previous triangle of ABP_* to ACP_1, and so the consumer surplus would be reduced to the small green triangle. From this, it can be deduced that rises in price will reduce consumer surplus, and falls in price will increase consumer surplus. An additional point to make is that with price rising from P_* to P_1, the area CBD represents deadweight loss, but if instead price fell from P_1 to P_*, then the area CBD would instead show the amount of new consumers entering the market.

Consumer Surplus Change Evaluation:

- For evaluating a consumer surplus change, write that it depends on the extent of the change in price and also the price elasticity of demand

2.3 THE NATURE AND CHARACTERISTICS OF SUPPLY

Supply – The quantity of a good or service that producers are willing and able to offer at different market prices over a period of time

Law of Supply – A law that states that, ceteris paribus, there is a direct relationship between the quantity supplied and price of a good or service

Supply Curve – A graph showing how much of a product will be supplied at any given price

Supply Schedule – The collection of data used to draw the supply curve of a product

Competitive Market – A market in which individual firms cannot influence the market price of the product they are selling, because of the high competition from other firms

Competitive Supply – When a firm can use its factors of production to produce more than one type of product e.g. a firm can use land to supply food or instead divert its use of land to producing bio-fuels

Composite Supply (Rival Supply) – When supply of a product comes from more than one source; a product whose demand can be satisfied through various sources e.g. electricity is a composite supply as it can be made from gas, nuclear power, wind turbines, hydroelectric turbines etc... All these sources contribute to make up the supply of electricity, and thus the demand for electricity can be satisfied through the supply of gas, nuclear power etc... There is competition between them and so the most economical source is used first (and used the most), but in the end the rest are combined to co-operate and contribute to the supply of said product

Joint Supply – When a firm can produce more than one type of product with roughly the same factors of production e.g. the supply of beef and leather are linked because both of them are made using cows

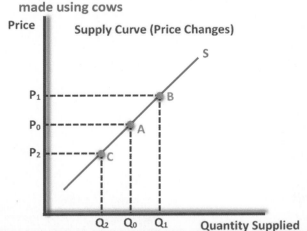

Supply Curve (Price Changes)

On the diagram to the left, the y-axis is labelled 'Price' in reference to the price of a particular product (e.g. it could be the price of a coke can), and the x-axis is labelled 'Quantity Supplied' in reference to the units supplied of the same particular product. At price P_0 (some arbitrary price such as £1.00, for example) the quantity supplied of the product is Q_0 (some arbitrary amount such as 2 units), shown by point A on the supply curve (S). The supply curve can be used to show what is expected to happen to the quantity supplied of a product when its price changes.

If the price of said product increases from P_0 to P_1, the diagram shows that the quantity supplied of the product should increase from Q_0 to Q_1, shown by moving from point A to point B. This makes intuitive sense as a firm will want to supply more of a product if its price is higher (potential for higher return). This movement along the supply curve is known as an extension of supply. Conversely, if the price of said product decreases from P_0 to P_2, the diagram shows that the quantity supplied of the product should decrease from Q_0 to Q_2, shown by moving from point A to point C. This makes intuitive sense as a firm will have less incentive to supply a product if its price is lower (potential for return is lower). This movement along the supply curve is known as a contraction of supply.

Why the Supply Curve is Upwards Sloping:

- There are 3 reasons as to why the supply curve is thought to be upwards sloping:
  - The profit motive
  - Production and costs
  - New suppliers / entrants coming into the market
- **The profit motive**
  - When the price of a product rises, it becomes more profitable for businesses to increase their output as they can increase their potential return
- **Production and costs**
  - When a firm increases output, this tends to lead to an increase in said firm's costs of production, and so a higher price is needed to cover these extra costs of production
  - This is partially due to what is known as the law of marginal diminishing returns. In the short run, it is usually not possible to change the quantity of capital. As a result, as a larger and larger amount of workers are combined with a fixed stock of capital, workers begin to get overcrowded, resulting in workers getting in each other's way. This means that as they add workers, output will still increase but it will require proportionally more and more workers to do so. This leads to their marginal cost of production rising, and so they are likely to raise the price in order to cover this
- **New suppliers / entrants coming into the market**
  - Higher prices in a market can incentivise other firms / suppliers to enter the market, leading to an increase in quantity supplied as more firms are willing and able to supply a given product in a given time period

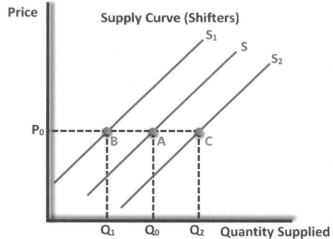

Whilst we have looked at price changes and what they do to the quantity supplied of a product, it is also important to look at non-price factors and how they can have an effect on the quantity supplied of a product. If there is say, a decrease in the total number of suppliers (possibly due to some going out of business), the total amount of firms willing and able to supply a given product (e.g. a can of coke) will decrease, resulting in supply decreasing (shifting to the left) from S to S_1. This results in the same price of the product (P_0), resulting in a lower quantity supplied of the product (Q_1, rather than Q_0), simply due to the fall in overall supply.

Conversely, if, for example, there is a decrease in the cost of a resource (e.g. aluminium) necessary for the production of a product (e.g. airplanes) then it is likely that the total amount of firms willing and able to supply said product would increase, due to the fact that they can produce more output with the same value of costs (e.g. if a firm has £100 to spend on a resource and the cost of said resource falls, this means that they can get more of the necessary resource with the same £100). As a consequence, the increase in supply (shift to the right) from S to S_2 can result in the same price of the product (P_0) leading to a higher quantity supplied of the product (Q_2, rather than Q_0), simply due to the increase in overall supply. There are several non-price factors which have these effects (these will be listed on the following page).

PRATNESTS (Supply Shifters / Determinants / Conditions):

P – Productivity – If productivity changes, this will lead to a change in output per worker. If you think about the formula of average costs [$Average\ Costs = \frac{Total\ Costs}{Output}$], an increase, for example, in the level of output, with no change in total costs (as you have the same number of workers), will cause the firm's average costs of production to decrease (a constant number divided by a larger number, results in a smaller final number). Lower average costs of production should mean that firms experiencing the rise in productivity will be able to supply more at any given price **e.g. increase in productivity → decrease in average cost of production → increase in supply NOTE – Technically speaking it is possible that a firm's raw material costs, for example, could increase if there is higher output per worker, but the general idea is that the change in total costs will be a lot smaller than the change in total output (caused by the increased output per worker), resulting in the reduced average costs of production**

R – Resource Costs – If, for example, there is a fall in the cost of one of the factors of production, ceteris paribus, this will lead to a reduction in firms' costs of production, allowing them to supply more at any given price **e.g. reduction in the cost of steel, or reduction in wage costs → decrease in cost of production → increase in supply**

A – Alternative Output – If a firm has joint supply, then an increase in the price of product Y may lead to a fall in the supply of product X, as it would now be more profitable to produce product Y and so the firm would likely reduce its supply of product X **e.g. increase in price of trucks → vehicle production firm increasing quantity supplied of trucks → less spare capacity for the vehicle production firm to use for production of cars → decrease in supply of cars**

T – Technology – If there is an improvement in technology, for example, this may lead to the production process of a product becoming more efficient, thus resulting in an increase in productivity. The increased productivity should reduce average costs of production (as explained earlier) and so the firm should be more willing and able to supply said product at any given price **e.g. improvement in technology → increase in productivity → decrease in average cost of production → increase in supply**

N – Number of Firms / Suppliers – If there is a change in the number of firms / suppliers, this will mean that there will be a change in the number of firms willing and able to supply at any given price **e.g. increase in number of suppliers / firms → increase in supply**

E – Expectations of Future Prices – If there is a change in the expectation of the future price of a product, this will lead to a change in the current level of supply for said specific product **e.g. future price of product expected to rise → decrease in supply of said product. This is because the firm will want to hold back production and keep more stock so that they can sell it for a higher return in the future. Once the price actually rises though, the firm will then increase supply NOTE – This is more likely to occur with a particularly scarce or finite resource**

S – Subsidies – If a firm is subsidised (given money for free) by the government, for example, this will effectively reduce their cost of production. If, for example, a firm's cost of production was £1000 and the government gave the firm a subsidy of £700, then the firm could look at their costs of production as having fallen to only £300 (£1000 - £700 = £300). A fall in a firm's cost of production will make a firm more willing and able to supply at any given price **e.g. government**

subsidises a large percentage of car firms → decrease in cost of production for said large percentage of car firms → increase in supply

T – Taxes – If corporation tax (a tax on firms' profits) fell, for example, this would effectively reduce firms' cost of production as it would effectively be like the government giving the firm money (like the subsidy). This would effectively reduce firms' cost of production and so more firms would be willing and able to supply at any given price e.g. decrease in corporation tax → increase in firms' profit levels (which can be looked at, effectively, as firms' cost of production falling) → increase in supply NOTE – A similar effect would occur if the government decreased indirect taxes, but they are a bit trickier to explain and so I will explain that effect in chapter 3.3

S – Seasons / Weather – If there is a change in seasons / weather, this can affect the amount of a product that firms are willing and able to supply at any given price e.g. winter is coming → decrease in supply of bananas (because they are more difficult to grow in the winter, and so if the firm / supplier hasn't kept stock, they may have to decrease supply)

NOTE – Anything that affects firms' costs of production will result in a change in supply

Price Elasticity of Supply (PES) – A measure of the responsiveness of quantity supplied relative to a change in the price of a good or service

Price Elasticity of Supply (PES) Formula – $\frac{\% \ change \ in \ quantity \ supplied}{\% \ change \ in \ price}$

Price Inelastic Supply – Where the percentage change in the quantity supplied of a product is insensitive to a change in the price of the product (0 < PES < 1) e.g. if the price of a commodity, such as oil, increases, an oil company will be slow to increase supply as it takes a long time to drill oil out from the ground

Price Elastic Supply – Where the percentage change in the quantity supplied of a product is sensitive to a change in the price of the product (PES > 1) e.g. if a car factory is operating at 60% of full capacity, then the car company could easily increase the quantity supplied of cars if there was an increase in price, and so would likely do so, very quickly, and to a great extent, relative to the size of the increase in price

Price Unitary Elastic Supply – Where the percentage change in the quantity supplied of a product is equal to a change in the price of the product (PES = 1) NOTE – The supply curves on pages 37 and 38 are price unitary elastic supply curves

Percentage Change Formula – $\frac{New \ Figure - Old \ Figure}{Old \ Figure} \times 100$

PES Conditions:

- **Perfectly Price Inelastic Supply:** PES = 0
- **Relatively Price Inelastic Supply:** 0 < PES < 1
- **Price Unitary Elastic Supply:** PES = 1
- **Relatively Price Elastic Supply:** 1 < PES < ∞
- **Perfectly Price Elastic Supply:** PES = ∞

PES Numeric Example:

- Taking oil as an example, let's imagine that the price of a barrel of oil rose from £50 to £55, resulting in the quantity supplied of oil rising from 10,000 units to 10,500 units
- Plugging in the change in quantity supplied of the product into the percentage change formula, results in $\frac{10,500-10,000}{10,000} \times 100 = 5\%$
- Plugging in the price change into the percentage change formula, results in $\frac{55-50}{50} \times 100 = 10\%$
- Plugging these into the PES formula gives us $\frac{5}{10} = +0.5$
- The PES value being positive is what one would expect as price and quantity supplied always move in the same direction. This means that you will either have a $\frac{positive\ number}{positive\ number} = positive\ number$ or have a $\frac{negative\ number}{negative\ number} = positive\ number$ (for any of you who do A-level maths, this should be pretty clear)
- Interpreting this PES value leads to the conclusion that the PES for oil (which is sold in barrels) is relatively inelastic, or you could say that the supply of oil is relatively price inelastic. This is because 0.5 < 1 (which meets the 0 < PES < 1 condition needed for price inelastic supply)
- This tells us that oil suppliers are insensitive to changes in the price of the product, and so their changes in quantity supplied of the product will change by an amount that is small relative to the price change
- This would be expected of an oil supplier as it takes a very long time to drill oil out of the ground, and specifically to get the extra capital equipment needed to drill the oil out of the ground. Supply tends to be relatively price inelastic for all commodity suppliers, and house suppliers, due to the long production process **NOTE – On a side note, PED for commodities also tends to be inelastic. This is because they are often necessities and often do not have many substitutes (e.g. copper). What this essentially means is that if you are asked to draw a demand and supply graph (we will graph them together shortly) of a commodity, then it is best to assume that both demand and supply will be price inelastic, even if the question does not state it**
- If we instead got, for example, a figure of 2 for the PES value, this would be considered relatively elastic. For example, if the price of a product rose by 10%, the quantity supplied of said product would rise by 20%. This would be representative of the car industry, for example, where a car factory is likely not to be operating at full capacity (e.g. 60% of full capacity). This means that the car supplier can easily increase the quantity supplied of cars if there is an increase in price, and so they are likely to increase the quantity supplied of cars, very quickly, and to a great extent, relative to the change in price
- Examples could of course be done to show a unit (or unitary) elastic PES outcome, but I think with these numeric examples you should be well equipped enough to answer any such questions

LCN STS (PES Determinants):

L – Production Lag – The larger the production lag is, in terms of how long it takes for a firm to be able to increase output, the more price inelastic supply is likely to be. When labour is the most important factor of production, supply tends to be more price elastic as labour is generally easy to obtain, resulting in a small lag time. When capital is the most important factor of production, supply tends to be more price inelastic as new machinery needs to be installed and implemented into the production process, resulting in a long lag time. When land is the most important factor of production it will typically make supply more price inelastic if the product is a commodity that needs to be grown (e.g. agricultural / farming goods like wheat), but in some cases it could make supply price elastic if the land is quick and easy to obtain

C – Existence of Spare Capacity – The greater the amount of existing spare capacity, the more price elastic supply is likely to be. This is because such a firm will likely be able to increase output by simply hiring more workers to use the extra capital e.g. a car factory may be in this situation

N – Number of Firms / Suppliers – The larger the total number of firms / suppliers, the more price elastic supply is likely to be. This is because even if all of the firms were at 99% spare capacity, for example, if the price of the product being supplied increased, the combined 1% increase in production from a large number of firms will, on the whole, possibly allow a quick, large response of quantity supplied of the product (in the whole market) to the change in price. You can imagine that if it was just a few firms alone with 99% spare capacity, the overall response they could make would likely be quite small, and a lot slower

S – The Substitutability of the Factors of Production – The more substitutable the factors of production of a firm's production process, the more price elastic supply will be. If a vehicle factory, for example, has joint supply in that they can produce cars and vans, the substitutability of their factors of production will be important. If the price of vans increases, the speed and the amount by which they can increase the quantity supplied of vans will depend on how easy it is for the firm to switch production away from cars. If the capital required for cars and vans is quite different then supply will be more price inelastic, but if the capital required for cars and vans is quite similar then supply will be more price elastic. Similarly, if the workers making the cars are well skilled in producing both cars and vans then supply will be more price elastic, but if the workers making cars are very unskilled in making vans then supply will be more price inelastic

T – Time Period (Short Run / Long Run) – In the short run (the time period where usually at least one factor of production, usually capital, is in fixed supply), if there is a price rise, firms will be slower to respond to the change as they will have less time to make the necessary changes to their production process and/or production levels, resulting in supply being more price inelastic in the short run. In the long run, however, firms have more time to make said necessary changes to their production process (e.g. capital implementation) and/or production levels, resulting in supply being more price elastic in the long run

S – The Availability of Stocks of the Product – The larger the number of available stocks (of a product) that a firm has, the more price elastic supply will likely be. This is because they will be able to increase the quantity supplied of said product by simply releasing more of those stocks (from the warehouse, for example) of the product into the market. If a firm doesn't have a lot of available stocks, supply will likely be more price inelastic. This is because it will take the firm longer to increase the quantity supplied of the product as they will either have to wait for more deliveries of the product, manufacture more, grow more etc... which will take longer NOTE – Some firms cannot store stock of their products (the product is quickly diminishable). For example, hotels cannot 'store' extra hotel rooms (if a hotel room isn't used within a day, it is simply a wasted sale that has diminished), the amount of hotel rooms they have per day is fixed, at least in the short run, and so in such cases supply would be perfectly price inelastic

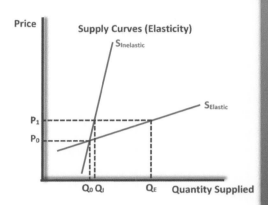

The graph on the left shows the difference in the responsiveness of quantity supplied of a product, when its supply is either price elastic or price inelastic. The price inelastic supply curve is represented by $S_{Inelastic}$ and the price elastic supply curve is represented by $S_{Elastic}$. The graph shows that an equal rise in the price of the product from P_0 to P_1, results in the quantity supplied of said product (when its supply is price inelastic) rising from Q_0 to Q_I, and the quantity supplied of said product (when its supply is price elastic) rising from Q_0 to Q_E. It is made clear, from the diagram, that the extent of the change in quantity supplied, relative to the change in the price of the product, is smaller with the price inelastic supply curve ($Q_I - Q_0 < P_1 - P_0$) and greater with the price elastic supply curve ($Q_E - Q_0 > P_1 - P_0$). Hence, it can be deduced that the more price elastic supply is, the more responsive the quantity supplied of a product is relative to a change in the price of said product.

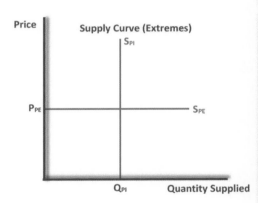

The diagram to the left shows some extreme cases of PES. If PES = 0 that would result in perfectly price inelastic supply (S_{PI}). This would mean that the quantity supplied of the product would be completely insensitive to changes in price, and so the quantity supplied would be fixed at Q_{PI} (this would likely be the case for hotel rooms, or seats in a theatre or on a plane). If instead PES = ∞ that would result in perfectly price elastic supply (S_{PE}). This would mean that the quantity supplied of the product would be an infinite amount (unlimited quantity) at the price P_{PE}. A perfectly price elastic supply curve is mostly theoretical, and so unlikely to occur in the real world.

PES Question Response (Guidelines):

- **Analysis:**
- **PES Coefficient** – Elastic, Inelastic or Unit Elastic?
- **10% Example** – PES = 1.5 (for example): Price goes up by 10% → Quantity supplied rises by 15%
- **Evaluation:**
- **Does the PES value correspond with economic theory?** e.g. PES cannot be negative, or the PES for oil producers should not be elastic in the short run
- PES values are **estimates and they may be unreliable**
- **Estimates can change over time**
- **Other factors can affect supply and demand**
- The analysis likely **assumes ceteris paribus which may not apply** e.g. supply could shift left due to higher corporation tax

Elasticities (Uses for Economic Agents):

- **PED** – Firms can use this to maximise total revenue by changing price accordingly
- **YED** – If a firm predicts that consumer incomes will rise by 5% next year, for example, and the firm is selling a normal good, the firm can now make sales predictions and possibly adjust stock levels. Additionally, if, for example, consumer incomes are falling and the firm is selling a normal good, a reduction in price could help compensate for the overall reduction in demand NOTE – Whether or not a reduction in price would increase total revenue, and thus help to compensate for a reduction in demand, will depend on PED
- **XED** – Firms can use this to calculate how many rivals they have, how close they are, and thus how to compete with their rivals in an effective manner. Firms can also predict and thus prepare for the knock on effects of changes in the price of complement goods
- **PES** – This has little use other than the fact that if a firm realises it has inelastic PES it can ensure that it makes careful investment plans. This is because market conditions may change by the time they have invested (bought capital) enough to increase output, and so money could be lost if they invest recklessly

Marginal Cost (MC) – The cost of producing one more unit of output

Producer Surplus – The difference between the price that a firm is willing to accept for a product and the price that they actually receive for the product

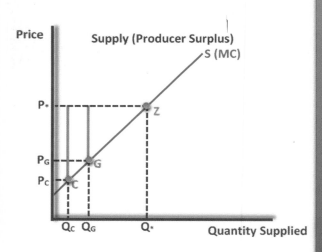

The supply curve represents a little bit more than just price and quantity supplied. Suppose that the price of a product was P_* with level of quantity supplied Q_*. P_* can effectively be looked at as the price that just covered the cost of the firm producing the last unit. Basically, if the price was even slightly below P_* this last firm (Z) would choose not to produce said product – this last producer (Z) is known as the marginal producer. To the marginal producer, P_* represents the marginal cost of producing the product – in essence, it is the price that reflects the individual firm's (Z's) willingness to produce the product, as it is the price that just induces them to supply the product (because it is the level at which it is finally profitable). This essentially means that the price at which a firm will decide that it is finally profitable to supply their product, is when the price is at least equal to their marginal cost. Hence, it can be deduced that the supply curve represents the marginal cost in a market.

Whilst we can see that producer Z supplied their product for the exact price they were willing to accept, it is true that, in a competitive market, every firm will sell for roughly the same price. As a result, there are other producers in the market selling for this higher price of P_*, even though they are willing to sell for less. Producer C, for example, is willing to sell their units at price P_C for some unknown quantity (Q_C includes the units that producer A and B are willing to sell, and so technically producer C is willing to sell $Q_C - Q_B - Q_A$ units, but this isn't shown on the diagram), but this price is lower than the actual price of the product (P_*). As a result, producer C is receiving a producer surplus of size $P_* - P_C$, represented by the left orange line. Similarly, producer G is also receiving a producer surplus, in their case, one of size $P_* - P_G$, represented by the right orange line. If all of the surpluses (through A to Z) were added up, they would sum to create the total producer surplus that firms in the market gain from producing said product.

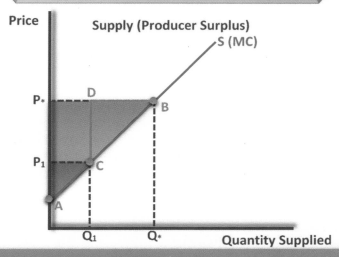

The total surplus is shown by the graph above. At a price of P* and a quantity demanded of Q*, the total producer surplus is the triangle ABP* (the letters have no reference to the producers from before, so you can label them as anything you want), which is shown by the small green triangle plus the bigger grey right-angled trapezium. Effectively, this means that the space below the price, above the supply curve and to the right of the y-axis, can be regarded as the total producer surplus. In addition to this, however, it is worth knowing that changes in price affect the size of the producer surplus. If price decreased from P* to P_1, resulting in quantity supplied falling from Q* to Q_1, this would lead to producer surplus decreasing in size from the previous triangle of ABP* to ACP_1, and so the total producer surplus would be reduced to the small green triangle. From this, it can be deduced that falls in price will lead to a fall in producer surplus, and rises in price will lead to an increase in producer surplus. An additional point to make is that with price falling from P* to P_1, the area CBD represents deadweight loss, but if instead price rose from P_1 to P*, then the area CBD would instead represent the amount of new producers entering the market.

Producer Surplus Change Evaluation:

- For evaluating a producer surplus change, write that it depends on the extent of the change in price and also the price elasticity of supply

2.4 MARKET EQUILIBRIUM AND THE PRICE MECHANISM

Free Market Mechanism – The mechanism by which the market forces of demand and supply determine prices and the economic decisions made by consumers and firms

Price – The sum of money that is paid for a given quantity of a particular product

Price System / Mechanism – The method of allocating resources via the free movement of prices

Market Equilibrium / Clearing Price – A situation that occurs in a market when the price is such that the quantity that consumers are willing to buy is equal to the quantity that firms are willing to supply

Disequilibrium – When internal or external forces prevent market equilibrium from being reached, such that the market is in a position where demand and supply are not equal

Surplus – An excess of supply (quantity supplied) over demand (quantity demanded)

Shortage – An excess of demand (quantity demanded) over supply (quantity supplied)

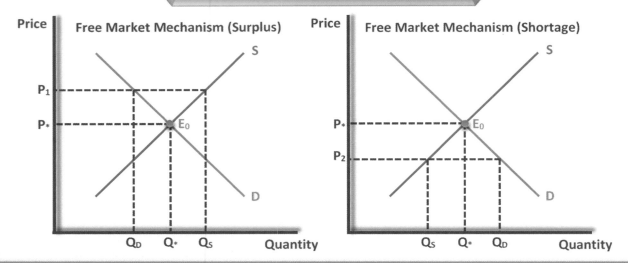

The two diagrams above show the price mechanism at work in a free market. Notice that the x-axis has been labelled 'Quantity' which means that the x-axis shows both quantity demanded and quantity supplied. Suppose that the price of a product was set above P_* at level P_1 (left diagram). This results in firms wanting to increase their quantity supplied of said product (potential for higher return), but results in consumers wanting to reduce their quantity demanded of said product. Firms will now be in a position where they have unsold stocks of the product. This has all happened as a result of the price being at a level that exceeds the value some consumers place on said product, and so those consumers are choosing to not buy said product. As a result, the most competitive firms will reduce their prices from P_1 to P_* in an attempt to reduce their stock levels, and those who are inefficient and cannot compete with such low prices will end up leaving the market. Supply will contract and demand will extend until market equilibrium (E_0) has been reached, resulting in quantity supplied reducing from Q_S to Q_* and quantity demanded increasing from Q_D to Q_*. The fact that quantity demanded and quantity supplied are now equal means that the market is in equilibrium, rather than the previous disequilibrium where there was a surplus of size $Q_S - Q_D$.

Suppose that the price of the product was instead set below P_* at level P_2 (right diagram). This results in consumers wanting to increase their quantity demanded, but results in producers wanting to reduce their quantity supplied (less potential for return). Some consumers will now find themselves in a position where they are unable to purchase the product due to some firms' stocks being too low. This has all happened as a result of the price being at a level so low that it is below the marginal cost of some firms, and so those firms are choosing not to supply said product. As a result, firms will increase their price from P_1 to P_* in an attempt to take advantage of this excess quantity demanded and maximise their returns (producer surplus). The higher price will also allow those firms whose marginal cost wasn't being covered, to re-enter the market. Supply will extend and demand will contract until market equilibrium (E_0) has been reached, resulting in quantity demanded reducing from Q_D to Q_* and quantity supplied increasing from Q_S to Q_*. The fact that quantity demanded and quantity supplied are now equal means that the market is in equilibrium, rather than the previous disequilibrium where there was a shortage of size $Q_D - Q_S$.

Derived Demand – Demand for a factor of production or good which derives not from the factor or good itself, but from the product(s) it can produce; demand for one item depending on demand for another e.g. labour is not wanted for its own sake, but for the level of output it can produce and what that output can be sold for

Unemployment – Occurs when someone of working age is out of work and actively seeking work

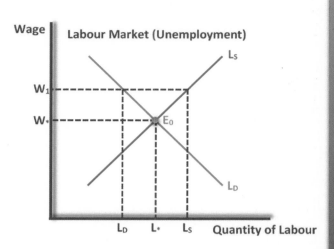

Labour can be considered to be a derived demand as labour is not wanted for its own sake, but for the level of output it can produce and what that output can be sold for. When the price (wage) of labour is low this tends to result in a high quantity demanded of labour, due to the potential for lower costs and so, overall, higher return (profit). When the price (wage) of labour is high this tends to result in a low quantity demanded of labour, due to the risk of higher costs reducing potential for high return (profit). For workers, the quantity of labour supplied tends to be high when wages are high, and low when wages are low, as the level of wages workers receive affects the amount of products they can purchase, and thus their objective of utility maximisation as well. As a result, labour supply (L_S) is thought to be upwards sloping and labour demand (L_D) downwards sloping.

Free market equilibrium will take place where the quantity of labour demanded is equal to the quantity of labour supplied, resulting in L_* number of workers being employed at a wage of W_*. If, however, the wage was set above the equilibrium wage, at wage W_1, this would result in the quantity of labour supplied increasing from L_* to L_S, and the quantity of labour demanded decreasing from L_* to L_D. This is a sign of disequilibrium, signalling that there is a surplus of labour as there are more people offering their labour than firms are willing to employ. This shows that there is unemployment of level $L_S - L_D$. This is known as classical unemployment and essentially means that workers believe their services are worth more than W_*. In such a case, the more competitive / willing workers (or those who don't value themselves highly) will offer their services for the lower wage of W_*, whilst those who choose to believe that their services are worth more, will leave the market. This would result in equilibrium being restored.

Exchange Rate – The price of one currency in terms of another currency

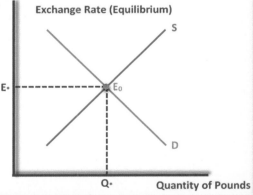

Anyone who wishes to buy any UK products (e.g. tourists, traders etc...) will need to use pounds to pay for them, and so the demand for pounds comes from foreigners looking to buy UK products (or assets). This is done through what is known as the foreign exchange (FOREX) market. If the exchange rate for the pound in euros is very high, the quantity demanded of pounds will be very low. For example, an exchange rate of £1:€5 (high exchange rate) versus £1:€1 would mean that Europeans would need to give up more euros for the same quantity of pounds (not appealing).

The opposite is of course true if the exchange rate is low, and so the demand curve for pounds is thought to be downwards sloping. This highlights that currencies (foreign exchange) are indeed a derived demand, as they are not wanted for their own sake, but for the products or assets they can buy. Moving onto the supply of pounds, pounds are instead supplied by UK citizens who want to buy products or assets from other European countries. This means that when the exchange rate for the pound in euros is very high, the quantity supplied of pounds will be very high. For example, an exchange rate of £1:€5 versus £1:€1 would mean that UK citizens could give up the same amount of pounds to get a larger amount of euros (very appealing). The opposite is of course true if the exchange rate is low, and so the supply curve for pounds is thought to be upwards sloping. If the quantity demanded of pounds is equal to the quantity supplied of pounds, then equilibrium will take place where quantity is Q_* at an exchange rate of E_*.

Interest Rate – The cost of borrowing money, and the amount paid for lending money (or saving)

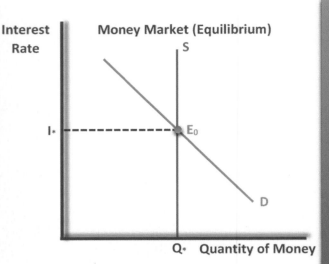

Money can also be thought of as having a market. The price of money can be represented in terms of opportunity cost, as instead of a person holding their money, they could purchase a financial asset, for example, to earn a rate of return known as an interest rate. As a result, the interest rate can be seen as the price of money. The demand for money is thought to be downwards sloping as a high interest rate means that greater returns are being forgone by holding it (as cash), resulting in a low quantity demanded of money. The opposite is of course true with low interest rates. For the sake of simplicity, we will assume that the Bank of England controls the supply of money and supplies a fixed amount of it, resulting in a vertical supply of money (S). When the quantity demanded of money is equal to the quantity supplied of money, the market is in equilibrium at E_0, where the quantity of money is Q_* at the interest rate I_*.

Comparative Static Analysis – Examines the effect on equilibrium of a change in the external factors affecting a market **NOTE – What we have been doing with the 5 previous diagrams is static analysis, whereby every factor that can shift demand and supply is held constant. Comparative static analysis simply allows for us to check more than one static equilibrium position to examine the effect on the market**

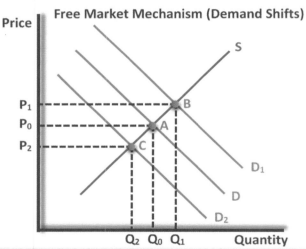

With this diagram, we can see what happens when there are changes in the demand for a product. If demand for a product rose due to one of its determinants changing (PRIEST ALI pneumonic), this would result in demand increasing from D to D_1. This leads to an extension of supply, resulting in the price of said product increasing from P_0 to P_1 with the quantity of the product increasing from Q_0 to Q_1. Conversely, if demand for said product fell due to one of its determinants changing (PRIEST ALI pneumonic), this would result in demand falling from D to D_2. This leads to a contraction of supply, resulting in the price of said product decreasing from P_0 to P_2 with the quantity of the product decreasing from Q_0 to Q_2. Hence, it can be deduced that, with both demand and supply present, an increase in demand will have an upward pressure on the price of said product and an upward pressure on the quantity of said product, whilst a decrease in demand will have a downward pressure on the price of said product and a downward pressure on the quantity of said product.

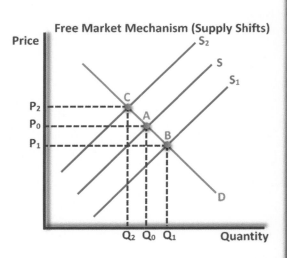

With this diagram, we can see what happens when there are changes in the supply of a product. If supply for a product rose, due to one of its determinants changing (PRATNESTS pneumonic), this would result in supply increasing from S to S_1. This leads to an extension of demand, resulting in the price of said product decreasing from P_0 to P_1 with the quantity of the product increasing from Q_0 to Q_1. Conversely, if supply for said product fell, due to one of its determinants changing (PRATNESTS pneumonic), this would result in supply decreasing from S to S_2. This leads to a contraction of demand, resulting in the price of said product increasing from P_0 to P_2 with the quantity of the product decreasing from Q_0 to Q_2. Hence, it can be deduced that, with both demand and supply present, an increase in supply will have a downward pressure on the price of said product and an upward pressure on the quantity of said product, whilst a decrease in supply will have an upward pressure on the price of said product and a downward pressure on the quantity of said product.

If both demand and supply were to shift at once, we would see that there would be opposing pressures on price, and possibly quantity, and so the final outcome would depend on the extent of the changes in supply and demand. This is why, for example, you could draw the same graph with demand increasing and supply increasing, three times, and have one with a higher price, one with a lower price and one where there is no change in the price. Essentially, what I am saying is not to be startled with price or quantity changes if both demand and supply are shifting.

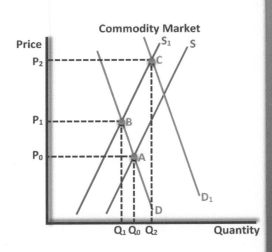

As explained earlier, both the supply and demand of commodities tend to be very price inelastic, giving the demand and supply curves the shallow shapes in the diagram to the left. In this market of copper, for example, the initial point is where S and D meet, producing quantity of copper Q_0 at price P_0 (world price). If the supply of world copper reduced as a result of a few countries' copper resources running out, this could result in the supply of copper decreasing from S to S_1. This causes a contraction of the price inelastic demand curve (D). This results in a small decrease in the quantity of copper from Q_0 to Q_1, but a proportionally much larger increase in price from P_0 to P_1. Possibly after this, China, and several other emerging countries, experience rapid economic growth, and so their demand for copper (which is needed largely for wires) could increase hugely, causing demand to increase from D to D_1. This causes an extension of the price inelastic supply curve (S_1), resulting in an increase in quantity from Q_1 to Q_2 and a proportionally large increase in price from P_1 to P_2.

As can be seen from the graph above, the price inelasticity of commodities' demand and supply causes the price of said commodities to be extremely volatile, and so changes in the demand and supply of them can cause huge price fluctuations. Other commodities, such as cocoa, that have to be grown, can be even more volatile, due to their dependence on weather which can result in glut (abundant) harvests and very poor harvests, which can shift supply frequently. Housing can experience very volatile prices as well as it has price inelastic supply (combined with a 'standard' demand curve), and so changes in demand can cause huge fluctuations in the price of housing.

Demand and Supply (Evaluation):

- **Measuring Problems** – In a lot of markets it is very difficult to measure the economic value of something, say a worker. For example, someone who sells potatoes can be paid depending on how many potatoes they harvest, but the value of a teacher or nurse is much more difficult, if not impossible, to measure
- **Government Provision** – Some products are provided by the public sector, such as education, health etc…, and so the government has large control over the pricing of those
- **Varying Objectives of Firms** – Firms may not be rational in that even if price is below equilibrium, a firm may choose not to expand as it would rather stay small. Additionally, in football, for example, Premier League football clubs often sell out all tickets before match day, hinting that they could increase prices higher than they do. The main reason they don't is because they would likely be criticised for taking advantage of low-income supporters, or even excluding them, if they raised the price

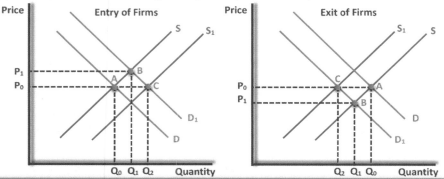

The graphs above show how changes in demand can result in the entry and exit of firms. Suppose that demand increased (graph on the left) from D to D_1 due to, for example, a rise in average disposable income. This would lead to an extension of supply (S), resulting in the price of the product rising from P_0 to P_1 and the quantity of the product increasing from Q_0 to Q_1. The firms currently in the market are now earning a higher producer surplus than before, given the fact that the price has rose (remember that price increases lead to rises in producer surplus). This can incentivise firms outside of this market to enter it, as the higher producer surplus makes this market look more profitable. If there happens to be no barriers to entry, then, in the long run, firms outside the market will begin to enter. This will lead to supply increasing from S to S_1 as there would be an increase in the number of firms. Firms will likely keep entering the market until the potential rate of return in this product market is no more lucrative than others, at which point firms will have no more incentive to enter the market. In this case, the extension of demand (caused by the increase in supply) happens to bring price back to the old price (P_1 back to P_0) and increase the quantity of the product further from Q_1 to Q_2.

The graph on the right simply shows the opposite occurring. If the price of a substitute to a product decreased, for example, this would likely result in demand for said product decreasing from D to D_1. This would cause a contraction of supply (S), causing the price of the product to fall from P_0 to P_1 and the quantity of the product to fall from Q_0 to Q_1. This fall in the price of the product would lead to a lower producer surplus, and so some firms may decide that the rate of return in this market is too low for them to wish to continue production. If there happens to be no barriers to exit, then, in the long run, incumbent firms (firms already in the market) will begin to leave. Firms will likely keep leaving the market until a point is reached, whereby only the firms that still continue to find it profitable will stay in the market. This will lead to supply decreasing from S to S_1, as there would be a decrease in the number of firms. In this case, the contraction of demand (caused by the decrease in supply) happens to bring price back to the old price (P_1 back to P_0) and decrease the quantity of the product further from Q_1 to Q_2.

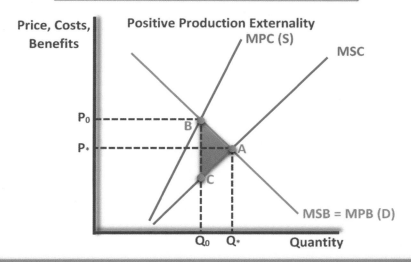

The graph above shows the effects of a positive production externality. Suppose that, next to a river, there is a water purification plant (chemical firm) located upstream, resulting in firms or consumers (third parties) experiencing a benefit as they can now spend less of their time purifying water and instead more time on doing other things (reduced opportunity cost). Additionally, those who didn't have water purification technology may now be able to use the water from the river without damaging their health. The private cost, to the firm, of purifying the water is simply represented by MPC, and the benefit to society is simply represented by MSB. However, it can be said that the economic decision of the chemical firm to purify the water has reduced the opportunity cost of firms (e.g. farms using the water) and consumers, with the added cost reduction of reduced damage to the health of those previously using the unclean water. As a result, MSC is lower than MPC as external costs have fallen (social costs = private costs (+) –the reduction in cost to society).

The free market equilibrium will simply take place where demand equals supply, resulting in a price of P_0 for said product (water purification services) at a quantity of Q_0 for said product. This can be said to be occurring due to the chemical firm, and the people who paid for the water to be purified, only caring about their private costs and private benefits. As a result, we can see that a market failure is indeed occurring due to the fact that MSB does not equal MSC at production level Q_0, but is instead greater than MSC at that point. This means that the allocatively efficient outcome is not occurring because in order for such to happen the quantity of the product would be at level Q_* at a price of P_* so that MSB = MSC. This clearly shows that there is a problem of underproduction as the free market outcome resulted in $Q_* - Q_0$ too little units being produced, highlighting the fact that the free market mechanism has not resulted in a socially optimal outcome and is allocating too few resources towards the production of water purification. It can further be seen on the diagram that any unit produced below Q_* accrues a benefit on society equal to the vertical distance between the MSC curve and the MSB curve. The green triangle ABC can be said to be the size of the potential welfare gain (or welfare loss depending on how you look at it), as it is the individual 'benefit lines' all added up.

Other Examples of Positive Production Externalities:

- **Building Infrastructure** – When a firm decides to invest in infrastructure that will improve the efficiency of transport and production for itself, it provides a benefit to other firms in the area who can now use the infrastructure for themselves, and also to residents who may now have better roads to use

- **Research and Development (R&D)** – When a firm invests in R&D it can potentially lead to new technology. Firms often try to protect their inventions, but in many cases new technologies end up being shared (sometimes through workers changing firms or through the internet) which can generate great benefits for society

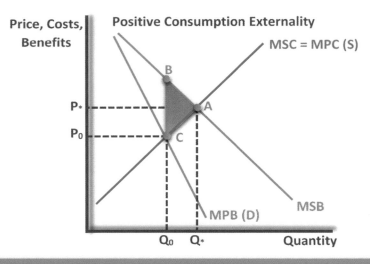

The graph above shows the effects of a positive consumption externality. Individuals in society, like you and me, consume education simply for our own private benefit. Many of us choose to consume and stay in education, in the hope that it will result in us earning better qualifications that will increase our earning potential (as we believe that our productivity will hopefully increase) and reduce our chances of becoming unemployed. Some may even consume education simply for the joy and pleasure of studying (less common), but the bottom line is that as consumers we are only concerned with our private benefit (MPB). What we fail or choose not to take into account is the potential benefits that our consumption of education could have on society. If you get a better job, and earn more income as a result, this will mean that the government will earn more tax revenue in the form of income tax receipts and so, as a result, be able to give out more welfare benefits, higher pensions, increase spending on health services etc... Additionally, education may also make us better able to innovate and produce new products that will benefit society. This means that the consumption of education has an external benefit, and so the social benefits must be higher than the private benefits (social benefits = private benefits + external benefits), which is shown by MSB being higher than MPB on the diagram above.

The free market equilibrium will simply take place where demand equals supply, resulting in a price of P_0 for education at a quantity of Q_0. This can be said to be occurring due to the fact that consumers (us) and producers only care about the private benefits and private costs. As a result, we can see that a market failure is indeed occurring due to the fact that MSB does not equal MSC at consumption level Q_0, but is instead greater than MSC at that point. This means that the allocatively efficient outcome is not occurring because in order for such to happen, the quantity of education would be at level Q_* at a price of P_* so that MSB = MSC. This clearly shows that there is a problem of under consumption as the free market outcome resulted in $Q_* – Q_0$ too little units being consumed, highlighting the fact that the free market mechanism has not resulted in a socially optimal outcome and is allocating too few resources towards the consumption of education. It can further be seen that any unit produced below Q_* accrues a benefit to society, equal to the vertical distance between the MSC curve and the MSB curve. The green triangle ABC can be said to be the size of the potential welfare gain (or welfare loss), as it is the individual 'benefit lines' all added up.

MARKET FAILURE AND GOVERNMENT INTERVENTION

Other Examples of Positive Consumption Externalities:

- **Health Services** – When individuals decide whether or not to get a vaccination, they do it on the basis of the potential private benefits and private costs of consuming it. The private benefit is that getting vaccinated reduces the chance of an individual getting a particular disease, but some may decide it is not worth the money, may dislike needles or have some concern about the potential side effects. As a result, the total consumption of vaccines may be lower than it should be, which means that there is a potential benefit to society not being accrued. This is because a higher amount of people getting vaccinated would benefit the rest of society by reducing their chances of contracting the disease (from the people who are vaccinated). Another view, is that the consumption of health services, in general, may lead to healthier workers, leading to an increase in their productivity and thus the tax revenue they bring in for the government (if they get paid more as a result of their higher productivity). The potential benefits are not being fully accrued, due to the fact that some individuals may not care much about their health and would rather spend their money elsewhere

- **Christmas Lights** – When someone decides to 'consume' Christmas lights, by putting them up, they do so on the basis of the private benefit they think they will receive from being able to look at their own decorations. It can be argued, however, that the total benefit to society is greater than this as passers-by and those living in the community will benefit from it. The potential benefits not being accrued here are simply due to the individuals caring only about their own satisfaction from putting up the Christmas lights they bought **NOTE – Potential welfare gain can also be seen as welfare loss. This is because you can look at it in the view that society has lost out on welfare they would have otherwise had, if it wasn't for the free market mechanism**

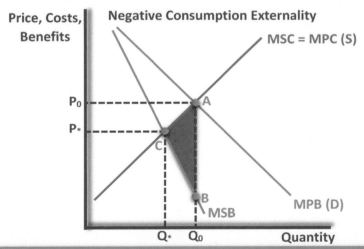

The graph above shows the effects of a negative consumption externality. Take the example of cigarette smokers. Smokers receive a private benefit, represented by MPB, due to the perceived utility (satisfaction) their smoking provides them with. This, however, impacts third parties (e.g. second-hand smoking) whose benefits are reduced due to the lower utility they can attain through, for example, simply sitting down due to their worsened health and decreased comfort. This means that the private benefit gained from an individual's consumption of cigarettes is higher than the external benefit (which is now lower), and so the social benefits must be lower than the private benefits (social benefits = private benefits (+) –the reduction in benefit to society), which is shown by MSB being lower than MPB on the diagram above.

The free market equilibrium will simply take place where demand equals supply, resulting in a price of P_0 for cigarettes at a quantity of Q_0. This can be said to be occurring due to the fact that consumers (us) and producers only care about the private costs and private benefits. As a result, we can see that a market failure is indeed occurring due to the fact that MSB does not equal MSC at consumption level Q_0, but is instead lower than MSC at that point. This means that the allocatively efficient outcome is not occurring because in order for such to happen, the quantity of cigarettes would be at level Q_* at a price of P_* so that MSB = MSC. This clearly shows that there is a problem of over consumption as the free market outcome resulted in $Q_0 - Q_*$ too many units being consumed, highlighting the fact that the free market mechanism has not resulted in a socially optimal outcome and is allocating too many resources towards the consumption of cigarettes. It can further be seen that any unit produced above Q_* imposes a cost on society, equal to the vertical distance between the MSB curve and the MSC curve. The red triangle ABC can be said to be the size of the welfare loss to society, as it is the individual 'cost lines' all added up.

Other Examples of Negative Consumption Externalities:

- **Playing Loud Music** – When an individual plays loud music, they do so taking into account only their private benefit, the benefit they likely gain from consuming loud music. This, however, reduces the benefit of their neighbours to gain utility (satisfaction) from, for example, watching TV or eating dinner. This results in the individual's private benefit being greater than the social benefit (due to the reduction in external benefit it causes), further resulting in a free market outcome that is not optimal for society, thus resulting in market failure

- **Getting Drunk** – When someone decides to consume excessive amounts of alcohol, they do so only taking into account their private benefit, the perceived benefit they will gain from getting drunk at a party, for example. This, however, can reduce the ability of others at the party to enjoy themselves and benefit from the dancing and music, if the drunk individual becomes aggressive and invasive, for example. It is also possible that if the drunk individual actually attacks someone, then the attacked individual has not only a reduced ability to benefit from the party, but possibly from consumption of future goods due to the damage done to their body (e.g. difficult to enjoy a drink with a busted lip). This ultimately means that the private benefit of someone getting drunk is greater than the social benefit (due to the reduction in external benefit it causes), further resulting in a free market outcome that is not optimal for society, thus resulting in market failure

3.2 OTHER CAUSES OF MARKET FAILURE

Private Good – A good that must be purchased to be consumed, and whose consumption by one person prevents another person from consuming it; such a good has excludability, is rivalrous (diminishable) and can be rejected e.g. a store owner can exclude you from buying a chocolate bar by not allowing you to have it if you aren't willing to pay a certain price for it. It is rivalrous (diminishable) in the sense that if you consume a chocolate bar, this affects the amount of the good (chocolate bars) available for others (if there was 10 units in the store, now there is only 9 units available for others, and now nobody else can consume that specific chocolate bar that you ate). It is rejectable in the sense that you can choose not to consume it

Public Good – A good that one person can consume without reducing its availability to other people, and from which no one can be excluded; such a good is non-exclusive, non-rivalrous (i.e. non-diminishable) and non-rejectable e.g. the government cannot exclude you from benefiting from the 'consumption' of national defence. Your consumption of national defence does not affect the consumption of others (if I build a house next to yours, we both equally benefit from national defence services). You cannot reject consumption of national defence because, effectively, just being in the country means you are consuming it

Non-Excludability – A situation existing where individual consumers cannot be excluded from consumption of a particular product

Non-Rivalrous – A situation existing where consumption by one individual does not affect the consumption of others NOTE – This is also sometimes called 'non-diminishable'

Non-Rejectability – A situation existing where individual consumers cannot reject consumption of a particular product

Pure Public Good – A good that has all of the characteristics of a public good

Quasi-Public Good – A good that has some, but not all, of the characteristics of a public good

Free Rider – Someone who directly benefits from the consumption of a public good, but who does not contribute towards its provision; when a person cannot be excluded from consuming a good, and thus has no incentive to pay for its provision NOTE – This is what makes public goods a market failure. The free rider problem means that people simply have no incentive to pay for the good initially, because they believe that they can just free ride off of someone else. As a result, it is likely that public goods wouldn't exist in a free market

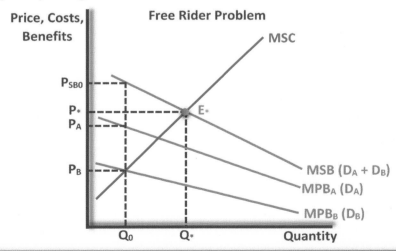

Let's take the public good, street lights, as an example. For the sake of ease, let's imagine that only two people in the economy demand the good, persons A and B. MSC simply represents the cost to society of producing the product, and MPB_A and MPB_B are effectively the demand curves of persons A and B respectively. At quantity Q_0, person A is prepared to pay price P_A for the product, whilst person B is prepared to pay price P_B for the product. These prices are effectively the value that each individual places on said quantity of the good, and so $P_A + P_B$ represents the social benefit, which is equal to the price P_{SB0}. As a result, MSB can be calculated at any quantity by adding the vertical sum of the two MPB curves, and so $MSB = D_A (MPB_A) + D_B (MPB_B)$. From this, we can see that the allocatively efficient quantity of the product is Q_* at a price of P_*, as that is where $MSB = MSC$.

However, if person A was to pay price P_A for the product, person B could just consume Q_0 amount of the product free of charge. Furthermore, we can see that person B will not choose to pay for the product at any point beyond Q_0 as they do not value the product enough to be willing to pay the cost ($MPB_B < MSC$ past Q_0). As a result, the free market mechanism will not result in the allocatively efficient outcome of Q_*. In a more realistic scenario, where there would be many consumers, we would likely find that none of the good would be produced. Every consumer would just wait in the hope that some other more desperate and/or more affluent person would pay for the product, allowing them to just free ride off of said person's purchase.

The free rider problem explains the reason as to why public goods are typically provided by the state. Politicians can talk about the provision of public goods in their campaign and, depending on the general response from the public (both verbally and in the form of the amount of votes received via the ballot box), the government can get a rough idea as to what extent they should use tax revenue to supply said public good.

Merit Good – A good that brings unforeseen benefits to consumers, such that it is likely to be underconsumed in a free market; a good that has more private benefits than consumers actually realise e.g. education, health etc… **NOTE – These tend to have positive externalities**

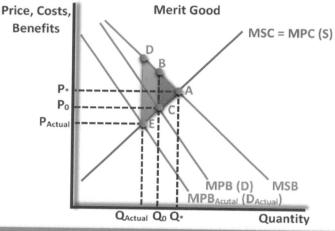

As a merit good is a good that brings unforeseen benefits to the private consumer, this effectively means that the consumer's MPB (their demand curve) is actually lower than what it should be (MPB_{Actual}). This is a sign of another market failure because it was bad enough that consumption of this good (education, for example) would lead to positive externalities as consumers only care about their own private benefits, but to make matters worse, consumers don't even fully realise the private benefit of education (causing the potential welfare gain / welfare loss to increase from ABC to ADE). This is like a double whammy, whereby you have one problem made worse by another. As a result, the price of the product (P_{Actual}) is even lower than it should be, and the quantity of the product (Q_{Actual}) is even lower than it should be. Most explanations of merit goods skip the line in the middle (MPB (D)) and so they may just have a particularly large gap between MSB and MPB (which on this diagram is MPB_{Actual}), but I think it's important to actually understand what is going on. One could argue that to solve the problem of the merit good, the government would need to increase MPB_{Actual} to MPB (e.g. increase information provision about the benefits of education), and then solve the problem of the positive externality (the ABC triangle) through separate means. They could also attempt to kill two birds with one stone by increasing demand by a very large amount. This may be rather confusing right now, but this should begin to make more sense once we start discussing the actual solutions that the government could take in chapter 3.3.

Demerit Good – A good that brings less benefit to consumers than they realise, such that it is likely to be overconsumed in a free market; a good whose consumption is more harmful than the consumer realises e.g. cigarettes, alcohol etc.. **NOTE – These tend to have negative externalities**

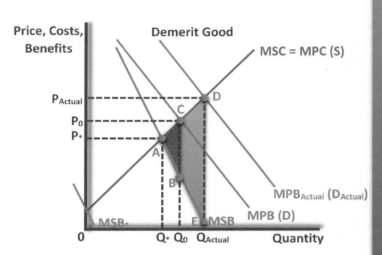

As a demerit good is a good that brings less benefits to the private consumer than they realise, this effectively means that the consumer's MPB (their demand curve) is actually higher than what it should be (MPB$_{Actual}$). This is a sign of another market failure because it was bad enough that consumption of this good (cigarettes, for example) would lead to negative externalities as consumers only care about their own private benefits, but to make matters worse, consumers don't even fully realise the lack of private benefit they get for themselves. People who smoke cigarettes, for example, will weigh up the costs and benefits of consuming the good, and it's by coming out with a net benefit that they decide to consume the good. The fact that cigarettes are a demerit good tells us that consumers are not factoring the health risks into their decision making, and so their net benefit (demand curve) is a lot higher than it should be.

Once again, this is like a double whammy, whereby you have one problem made worse by another (causing the welfare loss to increase from ABC to ADE). As a result, the price of the product (P$_{Actual}$) is even higher than it should be, and the quantity of the product (Q$_{Actual}$) is even higher than it should be. Same as before, most explanations of demerit goods skip the line in the middle (MPB (D)) and so they may just have a particularly large gap between MSB and MPB (which on this diagram is MPB$_{Actual}$), but I think it helps to actually understand what is going on. Once again, the government can decide to look at solving the demerit good problem and then the negative externality separately, or they can try to deal with both in one go. Once again, this will make more sense once we actually discuss the government intervention methods in chapter 3.3. There is, however, an additional point to be made about demerit goods such as cigarettes. The ways of solving the problem would remain mostly the same, but the additional point is that it could be argued that MSB should really be so low that the socially optimum amount of consumption would be 0 units (so that MSB would instead be MSB$_*$). If the government took this view, they would potentially opt for more extreme measures. Whether or not this is actually the case (that consumption should be 0 units) pretty much depends on your opinion and perspective of the situation (i.e. value judgments have to be made).

Information Failure – A lack of information resulting in economic agents making decisions that do not maximise welfare NOTE – Merit goods, demerit goods, asymmetric information, adverse selection and moral hazard can all be said to be examples of information failures. Additionally, information failure is, of course, another cause of market failure

Asymmetric Information – A situation in which some economic agents in a market have better information about market conditions than others; when information is unequally shared between two parties

Examples of Asymmetric Information:

- **Health Care** – You are forced to rely on the doctor's experience and competence. They ultimately have more knowledge than you and, as a result, could entice you to purchase treatment you don't actually need

- **Consumer Purchases** – When purchasing a computer at PC World, for example, the people walking around are likely to be on commission, or, at the very least, want the store they are in to make high sales revenue because that will likely lead to them being paid more. As a result, the staff around the store may entice you to buy computers that have specifications in excess of what you actually need, or, on the flipside, they may entice you to buy a computer that they know is not of good quality by pitching it to you in a better light **NOTE – The same is true in car dealerships, especially when second-hand cars are being sold. This is because the owners of the cars will have more information about them than you, and also likely be on commission**
- **Insurance** – You, as a consumer, know more about your circumstances than the insurance company selling you a policy. The insurance company, to some degree, is relying on your honesty and integrity

NOTE – Asymmetric information will either lead to the demand curve being too high (e.g. seller enticing you to purchase products you wouldn't otherwise buy if you had full information) or lead to a firm's supply curve being lower than it should be due to higher costs (e.g. insurance company paying out more money than they should be because of dishonest consumers)

Adverse Selection – A situation in which those who are at higher risk (more likely) of needing insurance, are more likely to take out insurance

Adverse Selection Example:

- Adverse selection can technically be seen as a type of asymmetric information
- Taking the example of a consumer looking for health insurance, the consumer will know more about their health history and whether or not they are very illness-prone or accident-prone
- This could end up meaning that the most likely people to take out health insurance are the ones most likely to become ill or get involved in accidents. This is because they know that they will be able to reduce their overall health costs (how much they pay for healthcare) by doing so, as they will be using the health insurance very regularly

Moral Hazard – A situation in which an individual who has taken out insurance is more likely to take higher risks; a lack of incentive to guard against risk where one is protected from its consequences

Moral Hazard Example:

- Moral hazard can also be seen as a type of asymmetric information
- Take, for example, a consumer who wears their helmet and drives their motorcycle around safely, one day, deciding that it would be a good idea to get health insurance, just in case they get caught in an accident that isn't their fault
- However, once they get the insurance, they may become lax and, as a result, become very reckless, driving around at higher speeds (because they know they are covered). Doing this, they are actually more likely to get into an accident and also be the cause of it
- The insurance company, however, won't know this and so when this now reckless motorcyclist gets into an accident, they will likely play it off (to the insurance company) as if it wasn't any of their own doing, possibly resulting in the insurance company paying for an individual who shouldn't have been covered

3.3 GOVERNMENT INTERVENTION AND GOVERNMENT FAILURE

Internalisation of Externalities – An attempt to deal with an externality by implementing an external cost or benefit into the price system

Government Failure – A situation where government intervention to correct a market failure creates inefficiency, does not maximise welfare and leads to a misallocation of scarce resources

Indirect Tax – A tax levied on spending on goods or services NOTE – This is unlike a direct tax, which is a tax that is typically levied on income or profits

Specific / Per Unit Tax – A tax of a fixed amount for each unit of a good or service sold e.g. £1 per kilogram of a product sold NOTE – Excise duty (taxes on cigarettes and alcohol, for example) are typically per unit taxes that are added on top of the overall ad valorem tax (VAT in the UK)

Ad Valorem Tax – A tax levied on a good or service, set as a percentage of the selling price e.g. VAT (20% tax rate on products sold in the UK)

Incidence of a Tax – The way in which the burden of paying a sales tax is shared out between buyers and sellers

Excess Burden of a Sales Tax – The deadweight loss to society following the introduction of a sales tax

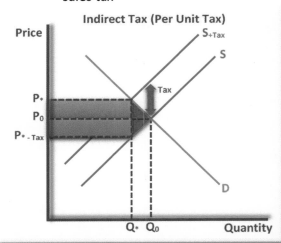

The graph on the left shows one potential method of government intervention to deal with negative externalities. The government may decide to impose a per unit (specific) tax on, for example, cigarette suppliers. This means that every unit will become some amount (e.g. £1) more expensive than it would have otherwise been before the tax. This results in the supply curve shifting left from S to S_{+Tax}, with the vertical distance between S and S_{+Tax} representing the size of the tax. This results in the price of cigarettes increasing from P_0 to P_*, and the quantity of cigarettes decreasing from Q_0 to Q_*. In this particular case, the size of the tax was completely accurate and so the shift in supply, caused by the tax, has resulted in quantity and price changing to the allocatively efficient levels.

There is, however, what is known as an incidence of tax. When a tax is levied on a good or service, the firm will pass some of it onto the consumer, but also take some of the burden on itself. This is because they don't want to deter customers too heavily by passing on too much of the tax. The difference between the initial price (P_0) and the final price (P_*) represents the increased price burden on each consumer purchasing a cigarette (in this example). This, multiplied by the quantity of units sold (Q_*), creates the orange rectangle which represents the tax burden on consumers. From the diagram, however, you can see that $P_* - P_0$ is only half the distance between the S and S_{+Tax} curves, and so it can be deduced that the leftover difference represents the 'price' burden on the firm ($P_0 - P_{* - Tax}$). This 'price' burden on the firm, multiplied by the units sold (Q_*), creates the green rectangle which represents the tax burden on firms. The sum of the orange rectangle and green rectangle represents tax revenue which, if spent wisely by the government, should contribute to a welfare gain for society. However, in the process we have lost some producer surplus and also lost some consumer surplus, and so there is an excess burden of the sales tax, a deadweight loss to society (the red triangle).

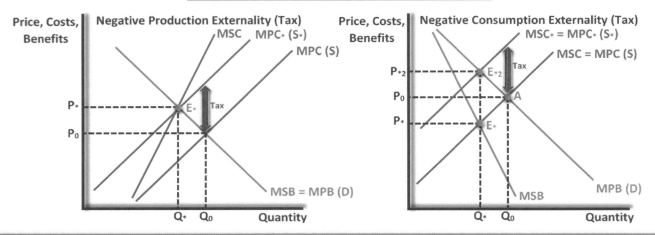

The graphs above show what would technically be happening on the externality diagrams. The one on the left is fairly simple, and it simply shows that the supply curve shifts left from MPC (S) to MPC* (S*) when the tax is imposed. This results in MPC intersecting the MPB curve in exactly the same place where MSC = MSB. As a result, the allocatively efficient outcome of price P* at quantity Q* is achieved. The graph on the right looks a lot more complex but is fundamentally very similar. When the tax is imposed, it results in supply shifting left from MSC = MPC (S) to MSC* = MPC* (S*). This graph differs slightly from the previous one in that it results in a new allocatively efficient price of P*2, as the price of the product (when attempting to achieve allocative efficiency) isn't what's important. What this government would be attempting to do by shifting supply to the left, is making the free market equilibrium occur in such a place that even though MSB does not equal MSC at said point, the quantity achieved ends up being the allocatively efficient amount (Q*).

You may now be wondering 'Which graphs should I draw then?', and technically speaking it shouldn't matter, however, when in an exam you would want to approach things in a wise manner. To address the demerit good problem first, I wouldn't bother drawing the 3 curves I showed earlier (where you had MPB_Actual), and so I would just draw MSB and MPB, where this MPB is effectively taking everything (the negative externality and demerit good problem) into account, mostly for simplicity and to save time. Effectively, I would use the standard negative externality diagram to just explain what the market failure is (the externality and, if it applies, the demerit good problem) and no more than that. I would then draw the 'Indirect Tax (Per Unit Tax)' graph (from the previous page) to show the effects of the tax and how it should help to achieve the optimal outcome.

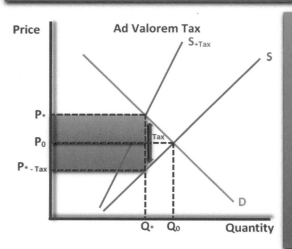

Generally speaking, when we talk about raising taxes on items like cigarettes, we are just talking about a per unit (specific) tax. If, however, you needed to talk about an ad valorem tax, this is the diagram you would need to use. The S+Tax curve is not parallel to the S curve, but instead steeper than it. This is because rather than adding some constant fixed amount (e.g. £1) to every unit of the item sold, you are instead multiplying the price of the units by a percentage (e.g. 5%). As the price of said units increases, this results in higher and higher increases in the final price after tax, making the S+Tax curve a lot steeper. The rest of the graph still works in the same way as the previous one, the only difference is that to show the absolute value of the tax, you need to draw the arrow right next to the tax burden box.

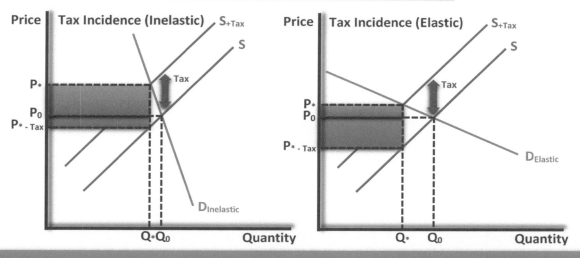

These final graphs simply show the difference in tax incidence depending on the PED. With the price inelastic demand curve, we can see that the tax burden on consumers is much larger than the tax burden on producers. Conversely, we can see that with the price elastic demand curve, the tax burden on producers is much larger than the tax burden on consumers. These effects occur due to the firm's knowledge of PED and how it affects total revenue. The firm knows that with price inelastic demand, an increase in their price (up to a point) will actually increase their total revenue, due to the fact that they lose a proportionately small amount of sales when they raise price as their consumers are very insensitive to changes in price. Conversely, the firm knows that with price elastic demand, an increase in their price decreases their total revenue, due to the fact that they lose a proportionately large amount of sales when they raise price as their consumers are very sensitive to changes in price. As a result, firms with price inelastic demand pass more of the burden onto consumers because it's actually beneficial for them, and firms with price elastic demand take on more of the tax burden themselves (allow their profit margins to take a hit) as they cannot afford to pass too much of it onto consumers (as the loss to total revenue would be very large).

Government Intervention – Indirect Tax Evaluation (Government Failure):

- **Difficult to Measure the Size of an Externality** – It is almost impossible to measure the size of an externality, and so it is virtually impossible for the government to know how large to make the tax. If the tax is too small, then the product will still be overproduced or overconsumed, and if it's too large then the product may actually become underproduced or underconsumed

- **Tax Avoidance and Black Markets** – If the indirect taxes are set too high, it may incentivise firms to avoid the tax, thus reducing the size of the decrease in supply and thus the reduction of the market failure. Black markets may also become more rampant as a result (people may buy them illegally across borders, for example)

- **Price Elasticity of Demand** – If PED is inelastic, then most of the tax will be passed onto consumers, and so the quantity of the product won't reduce by much, meaning that the overproduction or overconsumption will still exist and thus so will the market failure. Additionally, if PED is very elastic, then a firm may just decide to take on the entire tax burden, and so there may be absolutely no reduction in supply and thus no reduction in the market failure

- **Costs of Policing / Collecting Taxes** – It will cost the government money to police and collect these taxes, which brings with it an opportunity cost. Whilst the government may gain tax revenue from collecting the taxes, if they devote too many resources to policing and collecting, other public services may become neglected and so the government may become unresponsive to changes in public demand, leading to new problems arising. Additionally, the cost of policing and collecting will reduce the final amount of money they actually receive from the tax, meaning that the deadweight loss will be larger

- **Poverty** – Indirect taxes are regressive in that they take a larger proportion of income from the poor. This may lead to a worsening of poverty and make poorer people (especially those who have addictions) less able to purchase other important items such as merit goods, thus resulting in new problems being created

Subsidy – A sum of money given by the government to producers to encourage production of a good or service; a payment, usually from a governing body, to encourage production or consumption

Incidence of a Subsidy – The way in which the benefits of a subsidy are shared out between buyers and sellers

Excess Burden of a Subsidy – The deadweight loss to society following the granting of a subsidy

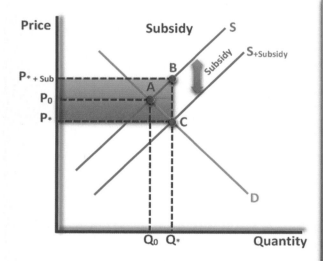

The graph on the left shows one potential method of government intervention to deal with positive externalities. The government may decide to give out a subsidy to health service providers on a per unit basis. This means that, effectively, every unit will become some amount (e.g. £1) cheaper than it would have otherwise been before the tax. This results in the supply curve shifting right from S to $S_{+Subsidy}$, with the vertical distance between S and $S_{+Subsidy}$ representing the size of the subsidy. This results in the price of said product (health care services) decreasing from P_0 to P_*, and the quantity of said product increasing from Q_0 to Q_*. In this particular case, the size of the subsidy was completely accurate and so the shift in supply, caused by the subsidy, has resulted in quantity and price changing to the allocatively efficient levels.

There is, however, what is known as an incidence of a subsidy. When a subsidy is paid to a producer, the producer will not pass all of it onto consumers, and so will take some portion of the total subsidy and just add it to its profits. The difference between the initial price (P_0) and the final price (P_*) represents the reduced price burden on each consumer purchasing said product, per unit. This, multiplied by the quantity of units sold (Q_*), creates the green rectangle which represents the total benefit to consumers. From the diagram, however, you can see that $P_0 - P_*$ is only half of the distance between the S and $S_{+Subsidy}$ curves, and so it can be deduced that the leftover difference represents the extra revenue (the revenue that the firm is just adding straight to its profits) that the firm is making per unit ($P_{*+Sub} - P_0$). This extra revenue per unit, multiplied by the units sold (Q_*), creates the grey rectangle which represents the total extra revenue for firms, the benefit to firms if you will. There is, however, a negative to all of this. Looking at the diagram, we can see that there is an increase in consumer surplus of size P_0ACP_*, and also that (using the initial supply curve) an effective increase in producer surplus of size P_0ABP_{*+Sub}. The entire area (the green rectangle plus the grey rectangle), however, is all tax revenue that is spent by the government, the cost to society of this whole endeavour. As a result, we can see that there is an excess burden of the subsidy (i.e. a deadweight loss) to society, as the size of the increase in consumer and producer surplus is smaller than the total cost.

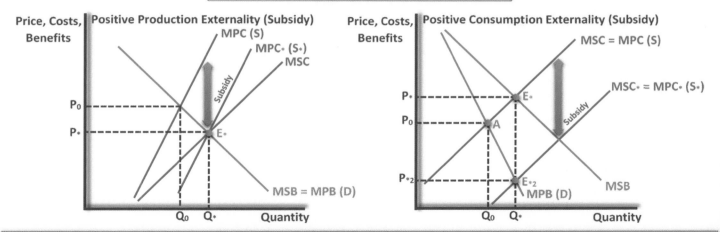

The graphs above show what would technically be happening on the externality diagrams (positive ones in this case). The one on the left is fairly simple, and it simply shows that the supply curve shifts right from MPC (S) to MPC* (S*) when the subsidy is granted. This results in MPC intersecting the MPB curve in exactly the same place where MSC = MSB. As a result, the allocatively efficient outcome of price P* at quantity Q* is achieved. The graph on the right looks a lot more complex, but is fundamentally very similar. When the subsidy is granted, it results in the supply curve shifting right from MSC = MPC (S) to MSC* = MPC* (S*). This graph differs slightly from the previous one in that it results in a new allocatively efficient price of P*2, as the price of the product (when attempting to achieve allocative efficiency) isn't what's important. What this government would be attempting to do by shifting supply to the right, is making the free market equilibrium occur in such a place that even though MSB does not equal MSC at said point, the quantity achieved ends up being the allocatively efficient amount (Q*).

Once again, I would suggest the same approach as before in terms of what diagrams to actually use in the exam. To address the merit good problem first, I wouldn't bother drawing the 3 curves I showed much earlier (where you had MPB$_{Actual}$) and so I would just draw MSB and MPB, where this MPB is effectively taking everything (the positive externality and merit good problem) into account, mostly for simplicity and to save time. Effectively, I would use the standard positive externality diagram to just explain what the market failure is (the externality and, if it applies, the merit good problem) and no more than that. I would then use the 'Subsidy' diagram (from the previous page) to show the effects of a subsidy and how it should help achieve the optimal outcome.

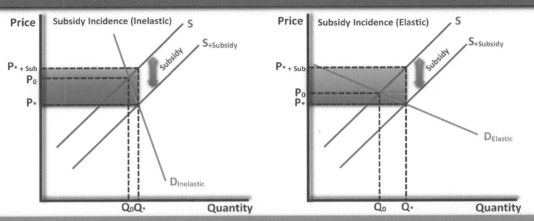

These graphs simply show the difference in subsidy incidence depending on the PED. With the price inelastic demand curve, we can see that more of the subsidy is passed onto consumers, whereas with the price elastic demand curve much less of the subsidy is passed onto consumers. In all honesty, there isn't any intuitive explanation I can give for why this is the case, and so you will likely just need to memorise these effects.

Government Intervention – Subsidy Evaluation (Government Failure):

- **Difficult to Measure the Size of an Externality** – It is almost impossible to measure the size of an externality, and so it is virtually impossible for the government to know how large to make the subsidy. If the subsidy is too small, then the product will still be underproduced or underconsumed, and if it's too large then the product may actually become overproduced or overconsumed

- **Price Elasticity of Demand** – If PED is inelastic, then whilst more of the subsidy will be passed onto consumers, the quantity of the product won't increase by much, meaning that the underproduction or underconsumption will still exist, and thus so will the market failure

- **Depends on the Firm's Reaction** – The subsidised firm(s) may simply choose to pocket the entire subsidy and add it to their profits. This would result in no increase in supply, meaning no increase in quantity and thus no reduction of the market failure. Additionally, it may cause some firms to become lazy and inefficient, firms that without the subsidy would have been wiped out of the market. In such a case, some firms may become dependent on the subsidy, and consumers may not receive a high quality product

- **Opportunity Cost** – Subsidies are extremely expensive, often costing billions of pounds. This is money that could have been spent on other essential services such as health services or education. Possibly, the government actually funded this through cuts in spending on health and education, and so they would be creating new problems in those areas. Additionally, if the government subsidy was paid for through borrowing, then the government will have to pay this back in the future, and they may do this by raising taxes (to increase tax revenue). This would reverse the effects of the subsidy by reducing supply. The subsidy diagram also shows that the size of the increase in producer and consumer surplus are smaller than the entire cost of the subsidy, resulting in an excess burden of the subsidy, a deadweight loss to society if you will, of size ABC

Regulation – The imposition of rules by government, backed by the use of penalties that are intended to change the behaviour of other economic agents to that which is socially optimal

Prohibition – An attempt to prevent the consumption of a demerit good by declaring it illegal

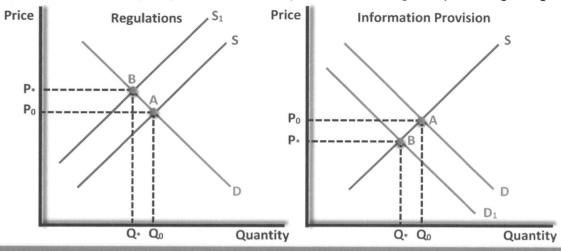

The above graphs simply show the effects of regulation or information provision, and how either of them can be used to solve a market failure.

Starting with the graph on the left, suppose that the government considers fast food to be a demerit good, and so enforces regulations that force firms in the fast food industry to reduce the amount of sugar and oil used in their food. This would likely mean that they would have to switch ingredients in their food to more expensive alternatives, leading to a rise in their cost of production. Additionally, firms that cannot manage to find suitable alternatives, or are not able to afford the more expensive alternatives, will go out of business. The resulting effect would be supply falling from S to S_1, further causing the price of said product to increase from P_0 to P_* with the quantity of said product falling from Q_0 to Q_*. This, in theory, could lead to the market failure being resolved. The graph on the right shows how the government could instead use information provision to solve the market failure. If the government implemented more education of the dangers of fast food into the public education system (assuming there is one) and also funded advertisements that talked about the dangers of fast food, this could increase the awareness of consumers to the point where they don't want to demand as much fast food. The resulting effect would be to cause demand to fall from D to D_1, further causing the price of said product to decrease from P_0 to P_* with the quantity of said product falling from Q_0 to Q_*. This, in theory, could also lead to the market failure being resolved.

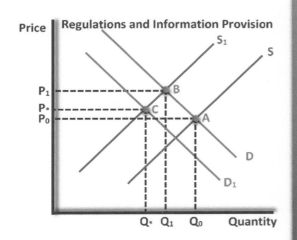

Regulation and information provision can also go hand in hand. If, for example, the government enforced regulation on cigarette companies forcing them to show pictures of damaged lungs on their packaging (we have that in the UK), this would first have the effect of increasing their costs of production as they would now have to print extra content onto their packaging. The resulting effect would be to decrease supply from S to S_1, further resulting in the price of said product (cigarettes) increasing from P_0 to P_1 with the quantity of said product falling from Q_0 to Q_1. The next effect would then be reduced demand from consumers who would now begin to better understand the dangers of smoking and what it could do to them. This would cause demand to fall from D to D_1, further resulting in the price of said product falling from P_1 to P_* with the quantity of said product falling from Q_1 to Q_*. The combination of regulation and information provision can be said to have eradicated the market failure.

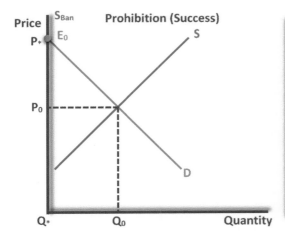

Another potential scenario would be one in which the government placed a ban on the production of a product (prohibition). This could occur if the government believed that the allocatively efficient quantity of said product was 0. This would result in the supply curve essentially becoming the y-axis (S_{Ban}), with the effect of increasing the price of said product from P_0 to P_* and reducing the quantity of said product from Q_0 to Q_*. Through this, in theory, the government would have solved the market failure. You may be thinking "Surely it's not that easy?", and that's because it's not. In reality, this just doesn't work, as will be shown with the diagram on the following page.

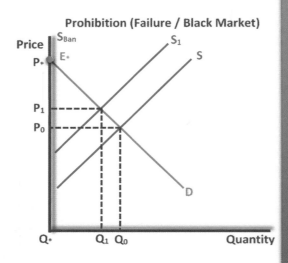

Prohibition (Failure / Black Market)

In reality, what ends up happening when the government tries to ban anything, is that they create a black market. You can think of the difference between S and S_1 representing the amount of producers who left the legal market. S_1 is made up of those who were already in the black market and legal suppliers gone rogue after the prohibition. This shifting in supply from S to S_1, results in quantity decreasing from Q_0 to Q_1 and price increasing from P_0 to P_1. The prohibition has succeeded in removing the legal consumers out of the market as $Q_0 - Q_1$ less units are being purchased, but the fact that there is still Q_1 units being sold shows that either some legal consumers have gone to the black market or were there to begin with (depending on the product). Quite clearly the prohibition has not worked and has actually just resulted in the hard-core addicts remaining in the market, willing to pay higher prices than they used to. As a result, the government could create more problems as said hard-core addicts may be willing to commit crime in order to be able to afford this higher price.

Another point worth mentioning, is that how far supply shifts to the left (i.e. how large the black market is) will depend on how dependent consumers are on said product. In America, they once prohibited alcohol and it ended in absolute failure with just about everyone turning to the black market. People simply didn't feel like they were a criminal when they consumed alcohol, and so they were willing to do it through illegal means. Suppliers knew this and so simply turned to the black market to supply their goods, meaning that there were very few suppliers who left the market. On top of that, the government only had about 1500 regulators to enforce the prohibition. What this effectively means, is that, in such a case, supply would have barely shifted left, because the size of the black market would have been so huge that it wouldn't have been that much smaller than the previous legal market. In such a case, a ban is unlikely to ever be successful enough for supply to turn into S_{Ban}, and so the market failure will persist.

Government Intervention – Regulation and Information Provision Evaluation (Government Failure):

- **Difficult to Measure the Size of an Externality** – It is almost impossible to measure the size of an externality, and so it is virtually impossible for the government to know how heavy to make the regulations or information provision. If it is too weak, then the product will still be overproduced or overconsumed, and if it's too heavy then the product may actually become underproduced or underconsumed
- **Opportunity Cost** – Regulation will need to be enforced which will likely be expensive and so bring with it an opportunity cost. This is because the money used for it could have been spent on other essential services such as health services or education. Possibly, the government actually funded this through cuts in spending on health and education, and so they would be creating new problems in those areas. There is also an opportunity cost if they are using the time of the police to enforce said regulations when they could instead be using their time for arguably more severe crimes. Crime rates could even go up as a result of individuals realising that police forces are being spread too thin
- **PED and/or PES** – If PED and/or PES is inelastic, then any decrease in supply or demand won't cause the quantity of the product to decrease by much, meaning that the overproduction or overconsumption will still exist and thus so will the market failure
  NOTE – If the information provision was positive (e.g. adverts about the benefits of

education) then the effects would be similar, just that demand would be increasing, but the quantity would be a small amount and so the underconsumption would still occur

- **Unresponsiveness** – If firms or people don't take the regulation seriously, or the proposed regulation has too severe an impact on basic freedom, people may just continue to behave in exactly the same way as before and so the market failure will not be resolved. In the most extreme cases, black markets may simply develop. Consumers may also not be responsive to information provision, and so, once again, the market failure will persist as there would be no or little change in demand
- **Difficult to Enforce Regulation** – Knowing whether or not a fast food company is using sugar in their food, for example, will likely be very difficult to enforce without becoming heavily invasive, and even then it may still be a challenge

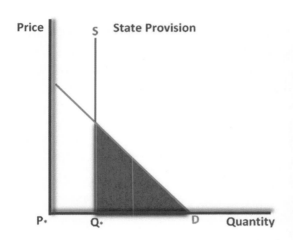

The graph to the left shows how the government may go about dealing with the underconsumption of a merit good like education, for example. With state provision, the government will supply all of the resources of said product, a fixed amount of S. When the government provides services (e.g. NHS, education etc..), it typically does so free at the point of consumption (it does technically cost people in that it comes from tax revenue, but at the point of consumption it is free), and so P* is equal to 0, resulting in Q* quantity of the product (the allocatively efficient level). The good points about this are that not only can it possibly achieve an allocatively efficient quantity, but it can do so in such a way that there is no price exclusion and so that all social benefits are considered.

Government Intervention – State Provision Evaluation (Government Failure):

- **Difficult to Measure the Size of an Externality** – It is almost impossible to measure the size of an externality, and so it is virtually impossible for the government to know how much of the product to supply. If the supply is too low, then the product will still be underproduced or underconsumed, and if it's too high then the product may actually become overproduced or overconsumed
- **Opportunity Cost** – State provision is extremely expensive, often costing billions of pounds. This is money that could have been spent on other essential services (depending on which product was being supplied via state provision) such as health services, education, transport etc... Possibly, the government actually funded this through cuts in spending in these areas, and so they would be creating new problems in said areas. Additionally, if the state provision is paid for through borrowing, then the government will have to pay this back in the future, and they may do this by raising taxes (to increase tax revenue). Raising taxes could have unintended consequences on the production and/or consumption of other merit goods in the economy. All of this is made worse by the fact that governments have a tendency to be very wasteful and inefficient as they do not have a profit incentive (or lack the incentive not to make a loss)
- **Shortages** – As can be seen on the state provision diagram, the red triangle represents the excess demand in the economy. This will have to be rationed through waiting lists, severity of situation, picking at random etc... Any of these methods is likely to either

reduce the total benefit of the product being provided to people (e.g. people's health conditions worsening while on the waiting list for the NHS), and will likely be heavily dependent upon value judgements from government officials

- **Ignores the Private Sector** – State provision completely discounts the ability of the private sector to provide any help in the supplying of the provided product. It is likely that the private sector would be more efficient and be able to provide the product at a lower cost. This raises the argument that if the government provides the particular product, they should do so in tandem with the private sector. It could also be argued that certain aspects of health services, for example, such as cosmetic surgery and dental implants, aren't actually merit goods and so should really just be provided by the private sector

Minimum Wage – A system designed to protect the low paid by setting a minimum wage rate that employers are obliged to offer to workers

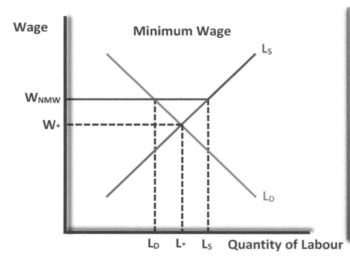

The graph to the left shows the effects of a minimum wage on a labour market. If left to free market forces, the equilibrium outcome would result in a wage of W_* with L_* quantity of labour employed. Suppose that the government now comes to the stance that W_* is not the allocatively efficient level, but that the optimum level is indeed much higher. The government could impose a national minimum wage (NMW) of level W_{NMW} on the market. This results in the wage being higher, however, there would be unemployment of $L_S - L_D$ as a result, likely an unintended by-product of the proposed price control.

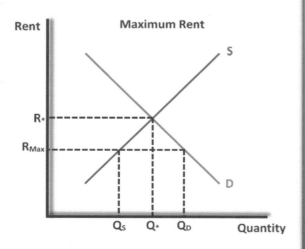

The graph to the left shows the effects of a maximum rent on the rented accommodation market. If left to free market forces, the equilibrium outcome would result in a rent of R_* with Q_* quantity of rented accommodation. Suppose that the government now comes to the stance that R_* is not the allocatively efficient level and that it is indeed too high a price for those on low incomes to afford, which is unfair as it could be considered a necessity. The government could impose a maximum rent of level R_{Max} on the market. This results in the rent being lower, however, quantity supplied will fall due to the potential return to landlords falling, and quantity demanded will increase as a result of the lower price being more enticing. As a result, there is a shortage (excess demand) of size $Q_D - Q_S$, and so on the whole there is less rented accommodation available and more homeless people, likely an unintended by-product of this proposed price control.

NOTE – The minimum wage and maximum rent diagrams can be used to draw minimum price (i.e. price floor) and maximum price (i.e. price ceiling) diagrams for everyday products. The only difference is that the axis would need to be labelled differently (price and quantity, rather than wage and quantity of labour, for example)

Tradeable Pollution Permits – Permits that allow their owners to pollute up to some given amount (decided by the government), and, if unused or only partially used, can also be sold to other polluters

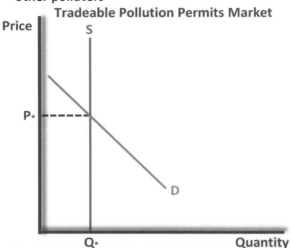

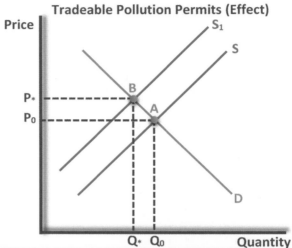

The above graphs show the mechanics of a tradeable pollution permits system. In attempting to reduce pollution driven negative externalities, governments can often find that taxes and regulation alone are largely ineffective. Tradeable pollution permits provide a potentially more effective solution to solve such negative externalities.

The system starts with the government first deciding on the level of pollution that they believe to be acceptable, which they then use as a barometer for the amount of pollution permits they will issue to firms. The diagram on the left shows the separate market that is created by the government. The government supplies a fixed amount of pollution permits (S) leading to Q_* quantity of pollution permits and price P_* for the pollution permits. This will cause the market failure to be solved as the supply of permits has been matched to the optimum quantity of output (that would be on the negative externality diagram), and so now all that is required is for the product market to adjust to meet this lower level of pollution. As firms will need to match their level of pollution to the amount of permits they have, any firms that are producing levels of pollution above their allotted amount will have 3 options.

One option is simply to invest in research and development (R&D) and green technology, in the hope of becoming more environmentally friendly and thus no longer creating pollution in excess of their pollution permits. Another option is to buy spare pollution permits off of other firms who were either environmentally friendly before the pollution permit scheme, or who became more efficient after the scheme was initiated. The last option is for them to keep on producing above their allotted pollution permits, resulting in them having to accept a fine from the government. Whatever choice such firms (the ones producing too much pollution) decide to make, their costs of production will have to rise. These higher costs of production will cause supply (on the right diagram) to decrease from S to S_1, resulting in quantity decreasing from Q_0 to Q_* and price increasing from P_0 to P_*. This shows that, in such a case, the pollution permit scheme will have solved the market failure as the reduction in supply (this would be MPC on the negative production externality diagram on page 64) has caused quantity and price to change to the allocatively efficient levels.

Government Intervention – Tradeable Pollution Permits Evaluation (Government Failure):

- **Difficult to Measure the Size of an Externality** – It is almost impossible to measure the size of an externality, and so it is virtually impossible for the government to know how many pollution permits to issue. If the supply of permits is too high, then production (and thus pollution) will still be too high, and if it's too low then the government scheme may actually result in underproduction

- **Opportunity Cost** – It will cost the government to initially do the work needed to issue the pollution permits, and then further cost them to ensure that the tradeable pollution permit market is working smoothly. Enforcement will be necessary to ensure that the scheme works and so, depending on how many firms are forced to undertake the scheme, it will cost large amounts of money. This is money that could have been spent on other essential services such as health services, education, transport etc... Possibly, the government actually funded this through cuts in spending in these areas, and so they would be creating new problems in said areas. Additionally, if the enforcement and administration is paid for through borrowing, then the government will have to pay this back in the future, and they may do this by raising taxes (to increase tax revenue). Raising taxes could have unintended consequences on the production and/or consumption of other merit goods in the economy and so, in the end, there may be no net reduction in welfare loss in the society NOTE – It is also possible that the enforcement simply wouldn't work as it might be too impractical

- **Fines May Be Too Small** – If the fines are too low, firms will simply accept the fines and thus the fact that their costs of production may rise slightly. The fact that the rise in firms' costs of production will be quite small (due to the fine being too small) will mean that supply won't reduce by much and so neither will production levels, resulting in a persistence of the market failure

- **Geographical Distribution** – The scheme may result in levels of pollution being highly concentrated in areas where there are a lot of firms with large cash reserves. This would mean that while the composition of pollution (on an area by area basis) may change, the extent of the damage of the pollution to those living in the now pollution dense regions, may actually become more severe and life-threatening than when the pollution was disperse over a wider area

- **International Cooperation** – In order for a country to undertake this scheme, there would likely need to be a worldwide consensus that most major countries would be partaking in tradeable pollution permit schemes. If this didn't occur, and a country decided to implement this scheme in their own country despite the fact that their international competitors weren't undertaking such schemes, the effects on the country's international competitiveness, growth and unemployment could be very negative, and so such severe costs are likely not to be worth it. This would be due to the fact that such effects on the overall economy are likely to reduce the amount of tax revenue that the government receives, meaning less money for government spending on R&D, with the additional factor that such effects are likely to cause a downward spiral into further problems (e.g. high unemployment)

SECTION 2
MACROECONOMICS

4.1 THE FUNDAMENTALS OF MACROECONOMICS

Macroeconomics – The study of the interactions and interrelationships between economic variables in the aggregate (total) economy

Macroeconomic Performance Indicators (GIBE):

- Economic **Growth**
- **Inflation**
- **Balance** of Payments (this will be explored in more detail in chapter 6.1)
- **Employment**

Main Government Economic Policy Objectives:

- **Sustained and Sustainable Economic Growth**
- **Low and Stable Inflation**
- **Full Employment / Low Unemployment**
- **Satisfactory Balance of Payments Position / Balance of Payments Equilibrium on the Current Account**

Extra Economic Policy Objectives:

- **Economic Stability –** This is the avoidance of volatility in economic growth, inflation, employment and exchange rates
- **Greater Income Equality –** This involves the redistribution of income from high-income earners to low-income earners via taxation and state benefits
- **Protection of the Environment –** This simply entails protecting the environment from overuse and/or misuse
- **Balanced Government Budget –** This involves reducing the size of the budget deficit and government borrowing

4.2 ECONOMIC GROWTH

Gross Domestic Product (GDP) – The total monetary value of all finished goods and services produced in an economy over a specific time period; a measure of the total output, expenditure (spending) or income of an economy NOTE – The time period is usually a year

Real GDP – The total monetary value of all finished goods and services produced in an economy over a specific time period, adjusted for changes in the price level (inflation) NOTE – We are yet to discuss exactly what inflation is yet, but this term will be explored in further detail in chapter 4.3

Standard of Living – The degree of wealth, material goods, comfort and necessities available to a person or society

GDP Per Capita – The average level of GDP per person NOTE – This is often thought of as the average income per person (or per head), as GDP can be calculated through totalling the income in an economy

GDP Per Capita Formula – $\dfrac{GDP}{Population}$

Circular Flow of Income – The movement of spending, income and output throughout the economy

Physical / Real Flows – A way of referring to the flow of factors of production from households to firms, as well as the flow of goods and services from firms to households

Monetary Flows – A way of referring to the flow of money from firms to households (in the form of factor incomes) and from households to firms (in the form of consumption payments / spending on goods and services)

Injections – Additions of extra spending into the circular flow of income

Leakages – Withdrawals of possible spending from the circular flow of income

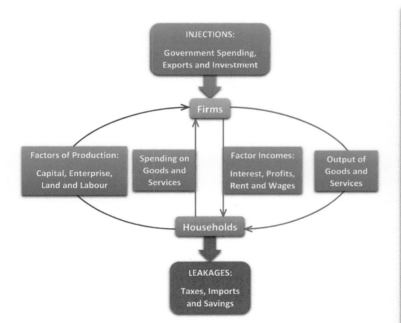

The diagram on the left shows a simplified model of how an economy works. In this simplified model of an economy, it is assumed that households provide the factors of production (which then provide factor services) to the firms in the economy. Next, these factors of production then earn factor incomes in the form of interest, profits, rent and wages, thus providing the households with income. Households can then use this income for spending on the goods and services that have now been created by the firms, and so the firms supply the households with goods and services in return for their spending. This diagram shows well that the total value of output of goods and services, total income and total spending, all produce exactly the same value and so can be used to calculate GDP.

There are, however, what are known as injections and leakages that affect the circular flow of income (the economy), which were previously ignored in the model. The injections into the circular flow of income are government spending, exports and investment, as they add to the total spending of an economy. The leakages from the circular flow of income are taxes, imports and savings, as they ultimately reduce the total spending of the economy. Both injections and leakages need to be taken into account when calculating GDP. It is unlikely that you will ever need to draw anything like this in an exam, but this diagram should help to explain the basics behind how an economy works. The importance of injections and leakages, and how they link to what is known as the 'multiplier effect', will be discussed in great detail in chapter 5.1.

GDP Measuring:

- Perhaps the easiest way to visualise what GDP is, is by looking at GDP as the total spending in an economy, which is represented by the following formula:
  - **Total Expenditure = C + I + G + (X – M)**
- The following list will explain the meaning of each letter:

- **Consumption (C)** – Spending by households on consumer products NOTE – This is like when you or me go to the supermarket to buy food, the sports shop to buy trainers etc...
- **Investment (I)** – Spending on capital goods (by firms) that add to the capital stock NOTE – This is when firms purchase goods like machinery, equipment etc... It leads to increases in the total capital stock of an economy
- **Government Spending (G)** – Spending by the central and local government on goods and services NOTE – This is spending on things such as education, the police force, infrastructure projects etc... This does not include transfer payments such as welfare benefits. Some portion of welfare benefits will show up under consumption when the unemployed, for example, spend their money on goods and services
- **Exports (X)** – Domestic products sold abroad NOTE – This is essentially spending from foreigners on products that are produced domestically (in the UK)
- **Imports (M)** – Foreign products bought from abroad NOTE – This is essentially spending by us on products from foreign countries like China, for example

- The reason that we add on exports is because they effectively represent extra spending entering the economy, whereas imports are like spending leaving the economy, as they are going outside into foreign countries, so we minus them off instead
- The combined amount of all of these components essentially gives us what is known as GDP, although it could be found by totalling up the entire income earned in an economy or the value of output produced in an economy
- Fundamentally, any of the measures will give us a rough estimate of the total monetary value of all finished goods and services, which in turn helps us to measure changes in the living standards of an economy
- This is because it is believed that a higher total value of goods and services suggests higher production of goods and services, and so a higher ability of individuals (like me and yourself) to purchase said goods and services and improve the quality of our lives

Informal Economy – Economic activity that is not recorded or registered with the authorities in order to avoid paying tax, avoid complying with regulation (because the activity is illegal) or due to laziness NOTE – This can even include trivial things such as unrecorded paid babysitting

Problems with GDP Measuring in Reality:

- **Output Method** – When using the output method, double counting must be avoided. An example of double counting would be counting the value of the output of raw materials, and then including them again in the value of the finished product
- **Income Method** – When using the income method, only incomes that have been earned in return for factor services (i.e. factor incomes) should be included, and so transfer payments (e.g. welfare benefits) should be excluded as they are simply redistributions of income and are not done in exchange for any goods or services
- **Expenditure Method** – When using the expenditure method, exports must be included and imports excluded (this can be somewhat challenging to do accurately in reality)
- **Informal Economy** – If there is a large informal economy, this can result in total spending being lower than it should be, thus resulting in GDP being lower than it should be (which can skew the GDP statistics)

Short Run Economic Growth – An increase in real GDP **NOTE –** Real GDP is used because it is essentially the more accurate figure to use for representing economic growth. This will make more sense after chapter 4.3

Long Run Economic Growth – An expansion of the productive capacity / potential of an economy

NOTE – Short run economic growth is sometimes known as actual economic growth, and long run economic growth is sometimes known as potential economic growth

Productive Capacity / Potential – The maximum output that an economy can produce

NOTE – If, in a question, Edexcel refers to 'economic growth' and does not specify whether or not they mean short run or long run economic growth, it would be best to talk about both of them just to be safe. Additionally, it is worth noting that the 'economic growth rate' means the annual (yearly) or quarterly (Q1, Q2, Q3, Q4) percentage change in real GDP

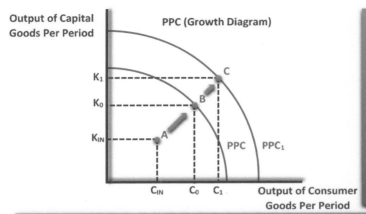

A PPC can be used to represent economic growth in an economy. An economy is thought to produce two types of goods: consumer goods and capital goods. As a result, we label both axis with the output of said goods. If the economy were to start at the point A, the output of capital goods would be of level K_{IN} with an output of consumer goods of level C_{IN}. This would be productively inefficient and would show that the economy is clearly not producing the maximum output that it can produce, hence the economy has not reached its productive potential.

Movements from any point inside the PPC to points that are closer to the PPC or on the PPC, show signs of short run economic growth, as they would clearly be showing an increase in the total output of said economy and thus an increase in real GDP. An example of this would be a movement from A to B, resulting in an increase in the level of output of capital goods from K_{IN} to K_0 with an increase in the level of output of consumer goods from C_{IN} to C_0. The PPC as a whole shifting outwards, such as that from PPC to PPC_1, shows that there has been an increase in the productive potential of said economy, as the maximum output that it can produce has now increased, thus representing an increase in long run economic growth. Bear in mind, however, that the economy could still be producing at B even if the PPC shifts outwards from PPC to PPC_1, and so it is not a given that just because there is long run economic growth that there will be short run economic growth as well. Essentially, the economy simply has an increased potential to increase output, but whether or not they meet that or get closer to it will depend on the situation. It is true, however, that in most cases when long run economic growth does increase, short run economic growth does tend to also increase with it (this will make more sense later). If such a case were to occur, this could be represented by moving from point B to point C (point B to any point in between PPC and PPC_1 would also show short run economic growth as well, of course). This would lead to the output of capital goods increasing from K_0 to K_1 with the level of output of consumer goods increasing from C_0 to C_1.

NOTE – The factors that lead to increases in short run economic growth and/or long run economic growth will be discussed in a lot more detail in chapter 5

Sustainable Economic Growth – Economic growth that can continue over time and does not endanger future generations' ability to expand productive capacity **NOTE –** This tends to involve increasing both short run and long run economic growth. Stagnant long run economic growth, and even worse, decreasing long run economic growth will ultimately limit the maximum output that the economy will be able to produce in the future. An example of this would be like if a country's government sold all of its oil and reinvested none of it back into infrastructure or education, but instead just wasted it on giving out more benefits or, in the worst cases, used it corruptly for their own financial gain (or to further their own political needs). This will begin to make more sense when we move onto the factors affecting long run economic growth later

Recession – Occurs when real GDP falls (i.e. when there is negative economic growth) for two or more consecutive quarters

Consequences of a Recession:

- **Lower Wages and Higher Unemployment** – The reasons for this can be shown using a labour market diagram:

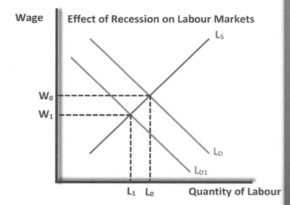

Wage

Effect of Recession on Labour Markets

Two consecutive falls in real GDP means that there must have been two consecutive falls in real output. Remember that labour is a derived demand, not wanted for its own sake, but for the output it can produce and at what value that output can be sold for. A reduction in output is going to lead to a reduction in the amount of labour needed to produce the remaining level of output, resulting in a fall of labour demand from L_D to L_{D1}. This causes wages to fall from W_0 to W_1 with the quantity of labour employed falling from L_0 to L_1. This represents a fall in wages and a fall in the amount of labour employed (i.e. higher unemployment as this would be happening in all different types of labour markets in the economy), and so are likely consequences of a recession. The potential effects of this are made more severe if some firms completely go out of business. Even for workers who don't lose their jobs, they are likely to see their hours cut (and thus become part time workers), resulting in lower overall incomes. Furthermore, if the unemployment becomes long term, this can lead to a further worsening of the damage (this is known as hysteresis and will be talked about more in chapter 4.4).

- **Falling Tax Revenue and Increased Welfare Benefits** – Firms are likely to make lower profits, resulting in lower corporation tax revenue for the government. Workers are likely to receive lower incomes and so the government is likely to receive lower income tax revenue. Additionally, overall consumption is likely to be lower, resulting in less expenditure tax revenue from indirect taxes (e.g. VAT). This lower tax revenue is not ideal, especially considering the fact that unemployment levels are likely to be higher, and so the government will likely need to increase their spending on welfare benefits as well. This will limit the amount of money the government can spend on services such as health and education, and may even result in cuts in spending in those areas. It is also possible that it could lead to the government borrowing more money. In such a case, the government may raise taxes in the future in order to earn the necessary tax revenue to pay said loans back, which is likely to have negative ramifications in the long run
- **Reduced Investment** – Recessions are likely to reduce the confidence of firms and so may result in them being more apprehensive to invest. This may limit the levels of long run economic growth

Benefits of Economic Growth:

- **Higher Standards of Living** – Rising real GDP, particularly real GDP per capita, suggests that consumers will, on average, have higher incomes and so be able to enjoy more goods and services, thus enabling them to enjoy higher standards of living
- **Lower Unemployment and Higher Wages** – Economic growth is likely to encourage firms to employ more workers, as higher economic growth means that firms will be producing more output and thus need more workers (you can show this on a labour market diagram with L_D increasing)
- **Improved Government Finances and Government Spending** – Economic growth is likely to lead to higher corporation, income and expenditure tax revenues for the government, and the lower unemployment means that spending on benefits will likely be reduced. This means that the government will have less of a need to borrow money and may also be able to increase spending on education and health services as well

Problems with Economic Growth:

- **Income Inequality** – Real GDP per capita rising only shows that the average level of income is rising, but it says nothing about how the income is being distributed. If the rise in average incomes was caused by the incomes of high-income earners rising rapidly, then it is possible that there may still be no improvement in the levels of poverty. This means that possibly only a small portion of the population will benefit, despite the increase in economic growth. Additionally, it should be noted that real GDP per capita will only rise if real GDP rises faster than the rate at which the population increases
- **Regrettables** – Rises in real output can occur due to increases in what are known as 'regrettables'. If, for example, the rise in real output has been accounted for by increasing the police force to match rising crime, people may actually feel worse off
- **Working Conditions and Negative Externalities** – Economic growth may not benefit people as greatly if it has resulted in them working longer hours and under worse conditions. Real GDP also doesn't include positive or negative externalities and so even if pollution rises, this won't do anything to affect real GDP even though people will experience a lower quality of life
- **Unsustainable Economic Growth** – If the economic growth is rapid and unsustainable, this may result in future generations being made worse off, as a result of an overuse and misuse of non-renewable resources, for example. Unsustainable economic growth is also likely to lead to high inflation, and so with that will come all of the costs of high inflation
- **Depends on Composition of Real GDP** – If real output increases but the extra output consists of mostly capital goods, people will not immediately feel better off, although they will do in the long run when said capital goods can be used to create consumer goods. In the case that the output mostly consists of consumers goods, people will benefit immediately, although they may forgo potential higher levels of output of consumer goods, as a result (as there won't be as many capital goods to produce consumer goods)
- **International Comparisons Can be Inaccurate** – If real GDP is measured in a country's domestic currency (e.g. the pound), when it is converted to another (e.g. the dollar) to compare economies, the final value may be unrepresentative (too low or too high) due to exchange rate movements which can be very volatile due to the speculation of traders

Gross National Income (GNI) – GDP plus net income from abroad e.g. net income from abroad includes things such as property income, taxes on producers and imports, repatriated profits etc…

Gross National Product (GNP) – GDP plus the value of output produced by domestic residents from overseas investments, minus the value of output produced within the domestic economy by foreign investors NOTE – The difference between GDP and GNP is that GDP includes all production that takes place within, for example, the UK's borders, whereas GNP includes all production that is produced by UK businesses, wherever the location. For example, if Nissan open a car factory in the UK, the value of their production (their output) will be included in the UK's GDP simply because the production is taking place within UK borders. The value of Nissan's production, however, would not be included in GNP as Nissan is a Japanese company (i.e. it is owned by Japanese people), hence why it would be subtracted in the GNP formula (this is because GDP in the GNP formula would have included it, and so in order for GNP to not include it, it has to subtract such values off). The opposite would of course be true if Greggs (a company owned by UK residents) opened a store in the US, in which case such a value would be added in the GNP formula

Purchasing Power Parity (PPP) – The exchange rate that equalises the purchasing power of two currencies by taking into account the differences in inflation and the cost of living between two countries NOTE – The purchasing power of a currency refers to the quantity of the currency that is needed to purchase a given unit of a good, or a common basket of goods and services. For example, the £:$ market exchange rate may be £1:$2, but due to differences in inflation and the cost of living in both countries, the purchasing power of the currencies may be different. A US citizen, for example, may find that bread costs $2 in the US, but then may find that when they convert their $2 into £1, the £1 they receive is not enough to purchase bread in the UK which is £1.20. This highlights the fact that there is a disparity in the purchasing power of the currencies as the market exchange rate is clearly not representative of how many pounds a US citizen should receive per dollar. This is why for international comparisons of GDP, for example, we use PPP adjusted figures (PPP is not calculated based on the market exchange rate, but through other means). This means that if we were to compare the UK and Japan in terms of GDP, we would convert the figures into US dollars (because the dollar is the standard currency used for such comparisons) based on PPP, rather than the market exchange rate which could produce inflated or deflated GDP figures for the UK, for example, and thus ruin the comparison

UK National Well-Being – Annual estimates of personal well-being in different areas of the UK. It is produced by the ONS (Office for National Statistics) through the use of surveys NOTE – The survey is known as the Annual Population Survey (APS) and is filled out by around 165,000 people. Personal well-being, and people's thoughts and feelings about their own quality of life, are thought to be an important aspect of national well-being. The ONS is thought to have done this in an attempt to look beyond GDP, and to instead measure what really matters to people. This is largely due to the fact that real incomes are not thought to be very closely related with people's happiness. This is because people's subjective perception of happiness will be related to a wide range of things above just their material prosperity

4.3 INFLATION

Price Level – A measurement of current prices of goods and services produced in an economy at a specific time; the average price of goods and services produced in an economy at a specific time

Inflation – A sustained rise in the general price level NOTE – If you imagine that, on average, the price of most of the products you buy increased, and in that same period of time your income stayed exactly the same, you can imagine the effect this would have on you. Effectively, this would mean that the same level of income (i.e. the same amount of money) would now purchase you a smaller amount of goods and services. This highlights the fact that inflation decreases the purchasing power of money

Purchasing Power of Money – The quantity a unit of currency can buy in terms of goods and services

Nominal Value – The value of an economic variable based on current prices, taking no account of changes in the price level through time

Real Value – The value of an economic variable, taking account of changes in the price level through time

Index Number – A number used for comparing the value of a variable in one time period with a base observation

Nominal GDP and Real GDP:

- Let's take an example in which nominal GDP rose from £100 billion to £102 billion over a year. This would represent an increase in nominal GDP of 2%
- However, imagine that the average price of goods and services (i.e. the price level) also rose by 2%, meaning that, on average, every good and service was 2% higher in price
- Such a scenario would tell us that there hasn't actually been any increase in the output of goods and services, but simply instead that all the existing goods and services rose in price, resulting in the value of the goods and services produced in the economy rising
- This shows that increases in nominal GDP can change simply as a result of existing products changing in price, which reduces the use of nominal GDP as we won't know whether or not there has been an increase in the output of goods and services or just a rise in the price of existing ones
- As a result, we use the following formula to calculate what is known as real GDP:
    - $Real\ GDP = Nominal\ GDP\ in\ the\ Year\ Being\ Examined \times \dfrac{Price\ Level\ in\ the\ Base\ Year}{Price\ Level\ in\ the\ Year\ Being\ Examined}$
- Real GDP takes into account changes in the price level so that we can exclude arbitrary changes in the prices of existing goods and services, and instead just focus on what we wanted in the first place (the change in the level of production of goods and services)
- Suppose that nominal GDP rose from £100 billion in 2015 to £102 billion in 2016
- For the price level, we use what are known as index numbers. Imagine that the price level was some random number like £80 in 2015. To use this value as an index number we simply decide that this price level (£80) will be our base year, and so we will now refer to our base year value as 100. There is no special reasoning for why we have chosen this year as the base year, we could have chosen any year, but we chose this one and we are now calling it 100 so that further years can be compared to it

- Imagine that in 2016, the price level rose from £80 to £84. This is a 5% change and so the index value for 2016's price level would be 105 (as 105 is 5% higher than 100). In reality, however, all of this £80 to £84 stuff is done behind the scenes, and so in reality (and in an exam) you would just be given the price level index numbers of 100 and 105

- Subbing everything into the formula, we get $Real\ GDP = £102bn \times \left(\frac{100}{105}\right) = £97.1bn$

- This (100/105) is reducing nominal GDP, as you can see that due to the fact that the price level has risen over the period, nominal GDP (the £102bn) is going to be multiplied by a number less than 1 (0.9523.... in this case). This results in the nominal GDP value being adjusted downwards to take into account the arbitrary rise in the average price of goods and services so that we can find out what 'real' GDP actually is

- The final value for real GDP in 2016 is then £97.1bn. If you do the same calculation for 2015 you of course get $Real\ GDP = £100bn \times \left(\frac{100}{100}\right) = £100bn$ which is what we should get, given the fact that 2015 was the base year. The fact that real GDP fell from £100bn in 2015 to £97.1bn in 2016 shows that the total output of goods and services actually fell, but the rise in their prices made it look as if economic growth had occurred when in actual fact it had not

- NOTE – If you are attempting to create real GDP values for several years (so that you can compare them), you must use the same base year for all of the calculations

Consumer Price Index (CPI) – A measure that examines changes in the weighted average of prices of a representative basket of consumer goods and services NOTE – This is used as a measure of inflation, and is the main one that is used in the UK

How CPI is Calculated:

1. A **base year is selected**
    - Ideally, this should be a relatively standard year in which nothing unusual happened. The variable being measured is given a value of 100 in the base year and other years are compared to it
2. The **ONS** (Office for National Statistics) **carries out the Family Expenditure Survey** (in the UK)
    - This involves sampling roughly 6,000 households, whereby they are asked to keep a record of their expenditure (spending)
3. **Use the Family Expenditure Survey to create a 'Basket of Goods and Services'** (this is just some long list of a set of commonly bought goods and services in the UK, which is roughly about 700 items in total)
4. The **products are put into different categories,** and **weightings are attached to them**
5. Weightings of the items are **based on the importance that said households place on the purchasing of the items in the basket**
6. **Weightings and items are changed each year** NOTE – This is due to changes in consumer tastes, often due to changes in technology
7. **Prices are checked in a range of stores across the country**
8. **Price changes are compared with the base year**
9. **The weightings are multiplied by the price changes**
10. **The weighted price changes are then totalled to create a value for CPI** NOTE – These CPI values can then be compared with preceding years to calculate the inflation rate year on year

NOTE – If you want to find out what the inflation rate is using index numbers, you can do it using the simple percentage change formula from chapter 2. For example, if the price level in the base year was 100 (2015), rising to 110 in 2016, the percentage change would be $\frac{110-100}{100} \times 100 = 10\%$ and so the inflation rate would simply be 10%

Retail Price Index (RPI) – A measure of inflation that is used for adjusting pensions and other benefits, to take account of changes in inflation. It is frequently used in wage negotiations as well NOTE – CPI is the one used for official inflation rates and, as stated in the definition, RPI only tends to be used for adjusting pensions and in wage negotiations

Difference Between CPI and RPI:

- **CPI** – CPI includes university accommodation fees and stockbrokers' charges which are not included in the RPI
- **RPI** – RPI includes all housing costs, including mortgage interest payments and council tax. It also includes the road fund licence and television licence, all of which are not included in the CPI

Problems with CPI/RPI:

- **Goods and Services Can Change in Quality** – It is possible that a good or service may increase in quality, leading to the firms providing said good or service charging a higher price. With CPI or RPI, however, it is possible that such a price rise may be seen as purely inflationary, and so CPI or RPI may not give an accurate representation of what is actually going on in the economy
- **RPI is Usually Higher than CPI** – This is because RPI uses an arithmetic mean whilst CPI uses a geometric mean. Those terms won't make any sense, but the bottom line is that it leads to RPI estimates of the inflation rate being higher than CPI estimates
- **Not Representative of All Consumers** – The goods which are in the basket of goods and services may reflect the general purchasing patterns of some people well, however, it may not reflect it so greatly for others. As a result, for these other individuals, the inflation rate will not be very useful to them as inflation could rise by a lot, but the prices of goods and services that said individuals purchase may have remained fairly constant
- **Difficult to Make International Comparisons** – If other countries are using different measures of inflation, comparing inflation rates between countries may not be very accurate
- **Basket of Goods and Services May Change too Slowly** – The CPI basket is changed once a year, but if people's spending habits are changing within months then CPI will be too slow to react. Additionally, the fact that some goods and services in the basket keep changing, may mean that historical comparisons will be less accurate
- **Data May Be Inaccurate** – Figures sometimes have to get revised simply due to errors in the collection of the data

Cost-Push Inflation – Inflation caused by an increase in firms' costs of production, arising on the supply side of the economy e.g. most firms use oil in some way, shape or form, and so if oil rose in price this would likely affect a large amount of firms' costs of production, resulting in them raising their prices to maintain their profit margins

Demand-Pull Inflation – Inflation caused by an increase in aggregate (total) demand e.g. If income tax falls, resulting in everyone, on average, having more disposable income, this will lead to a high increase in the demand for products in the economy as a whole. Firms may find that their stocks of products are running out way too fast, and so they are likely to raise their prices until people's spending on their products stabilises to a point at which their stocks are depleting at a steady rate. This can lead to an increase in the price level

Money Stock – The stock of money in the economy, made up of both cash and bank deposits
NOTE – Rises in this tend to lead to demand-pull inflation

Real Interest Rate – The nominal interest rate minus the inflation rate

Inflationary Noise – The distortion of price signals caused by inflation

Shoe Leather Costs – Costs in terms of the extra time and effort involved in counteracting inflation

Fiscal Drag – People's income being dragged into higher tax brackets as a result of tax brackets not being adjusted in line with inflation

Menu Costs – The costs of changing prices due to inflation

RUN MAF IS PC (Costs of Inflation):

R – Fall in Real Interest Rate – Higher inflation rates cause the real interest rate to fall and so, as a result, borrowers will gain and lenders will lose. If, for example, interest rates are at 6% and there is 2% inflation, a lender lending £100 would expect to receive £106 at the end of the loan period (£100 borrowed with 6% interest rate = £106 paid to lender). The real interest rate, however, tells us that he would only actually get £104 back in true worth by the end (real interest rate = 6% - 2% = 4%). This is because once inflation is taken into account, the £106 he will have would only purchase the equivalent of £104 worth of goods and services at the time the initial loan was made. This may make banks reluctant to lend money, or may mean that they will raise their interest rates (e.g. 10%). This may make it difficult for firms to borrow, resulting in lower investment and thus lower economic growth

U – Uncertainty – Inflation can create uncertainty about the future. If firms are uncertain about what their costs will be and what prices they will receive from selling their products, they may be reluctant to invest. Inflation also complicates household financial planning, making it difficult for people to decide how much to save and where to place their savings

N – Inflationary Noise – This means that market prices do not signal the relative scarcity of products efficiently. For example, without inflation, if the price of a TV rises, it can be concluded that it has simply become relatively more expensive (than other goods). With inflation, however, consumers will not know whether or not a good has become relatively more expensive or if it has just risen in line with inflation

M – Menu Costs – These lead to places like restaurants needing to print new menus on a frequent basis (due to frequent changes in prices)

A – Administrative Costs – Inflation can impose administrative costs on firms. Staff time may have to be devoted to adjusting accounts, assessing raw material costs, negotiating with trade unions about wage rises, and estimating appropriate prices

F – Fiscal Drag – The UK uses a progressive tax system, whereby when you reach certain levels of income (e.g. £43,000) any money earned after that point is taxed more heavily. If tax brackets are not adjusted in line with inflation, people's incomes will be pushed into higher tax bands meaning that the portion of their money above said tax bracket (e.g. £43,000) will now be more heavily taxed. As a result, more taxpayers will be paying higher proportions of their income in tax. This is seen as a cost due to the fact that as inflation rises, the purchasing power of money decreases which tends to lead to workers bargaining for higher wage increases to match inflation. Tax brackets should be adjusted to reflect the level of inflation so that people only get taxed more when they actually experience an increase in their ability to buy goods and services, not just when their wages need to artificially increase to keep up with inflation

I – Inflation Causing Inflation – Demand-pull inflation may be caused by inflation as households will expect prices to rise in the future, and so they may attempt to buy more products now. Cost-push inflation may be caused by inflation as workers will expect prices to rise, and so they may ask for pay rises in order to ensure that their real earnings don't fall. Firms expecting inflation may raise their prices in order to protect their real profit levels

S – Shoe Leather Costs – During periods of inflation, households and firms cannot afford to have their money sitting at home, not earning interest, as it will be losing value. They have to place it in financial institutions and have to search out the most rewarding rate of interest. For households the cost is their own time and effort, and for firms it is the cost and effort of their staff. Both of these carry large opportunity cost with them

P – Fall in Purchasing Power – Inflation increases the cost of living as people have to use more money to buy the same basket of goods and services. This means that the purchasing power of money will fall, although whether a specific individual's ability to buy products will fall, will depend on their income situation. If the inflation rate is 2% and someone's income rises by 2% (ignoring tax rates for simplicity), then such a person won't see a fall in their ability to buy goods and services. However, should someone's income stay constant whilst the inflation rate is 2%, this person will see a fall in their ability to buy goods and services. The bottom line is that some people are likely to lose out, particularly workers with weak bargaining power

C – Loss of International Competitiveness – If a country's inflation rate is above that of its main competitors, then the products that the country exports are rising in price faster than the price of the products they import. This is likely to result in a decrease in exports and a rise in imports

Hyperinflation – An inflation rate of over 50% a month

Disinflation – When the rate at which the general price level rises slows down, but still remains positive e.g. 5% to 3%

Deflation – A situation in which the general price level is falling (i.e. negative inflation) e.g. –2%

Disadvantages of Deflation:

- **Discourages Consumption –** When prices are falling, this encourages people to delay purchases of products because they will likely be cheaper in the future. This effectively means that you can increase the real value of your money by leaving it in a safe in your house (or in a bank), as the purchasing power of your money increases when the price level falls. This increase in saving can lead to reduced consumption (which can then also lead to lower investment) and thus lower economic growth

- **Increases the Real Value of Debt** – Deflation increases the real value of money, and thus the real value of debt as well. Deflation makes it more difficult for borrowers to pay off their debts, meaning that consumers and firms will have to spend a bigger percentage of their disposable income (or profits for firms) on meeting debt repayments. This can reduce both consumption and investment, and thus growth too
- **Unemployment** – In labour markets, workers tend to be resistant to nominal wage cuts, largely due to psychological reasons and the fact that they are used to getting annual pay rises. As a result, their wages are likely to stay constant at the very least. This is likely to increase the value of their real wages, but this means an increase in the real costs of production for firms. This may lead to firms laying off workers to cut their real costs
- **Deflationary Spiral** – As consumption decreases (due to higher savings), this represents a fall in overall demand. This fall in overall demand can lead to lower demand-pull inflation, causing inflation to become even more negative, resulting in a worsening spiral of effects

Low and Stable Rate of Inflation – Reasoning:

- The reasons that governments tend to want a low and stable rate of inflation is for the following reasons:
  - Firstly, rises in economic growth tend to be caused by increases in overall demand which, in most cases, will cause demand-pull inflation. As a result, government's will want to allow room for inflation that is combined with growth
  - Workers tend to like pay rises, even if these are only in line with inflation. This is simply due to the fact that psychologically people like to feel that they are appreciated and that their employers think that they are doing well, even if the pay rise is only in money terms
  - The previous reason means that firms can potentially get away with cutting workers' real pay and thus their real costs of production. They can do this by raising workers' wages by an amount smaller than the rate of inflation, which may provide extra profits for investment
  - The potential deflationary spiral effects of deflation can be extremely damaging, even when deflation is at very low levels (e.g. –0.5%), whereas inflation only really gets seriously dangerous once it begins to reach hyperinflation (above 50%)
  - The inflation rate still needs to be low, however, to ensure that international competitiveness remains high. This is so that exports will likely be higher, and imports lower in the calculation of real GDP, resulting in generally higher growth

4.4 UNEMPLOYMENT

Unemployment – Occurs when someone of working age is out of work and actively seeking work

Employment – Working age people who are either working for firms or other organisations, or are self-employed

Underemployment – Occurs when an individual is employed in a second-choice occupation, or is working part-time despite the fact that they would like to work full-time

Labour Force / Work Force / Working Population – The amount of people who are employed and unemployed, that is, those who are economically active

Economically Active – Working age people who are either employed or unemployed, and so are part of the labour force

Economically Inactive – Working age people who are neither employed, nor unemployed, and so are not part of the labour force e.g. discouraged workers, retired people, people (mostly women) looking after the home, working-age people in education (e.g. people in university), long-term sick or disabled etc...

Labour Force Participation Rate / Economic Activity Rate – The proportion of working age people who are economically active

Discouraged Workers – Working age people who would like a job but are not seeking one, as they believe that they would not be able to find one

Claimant Count – A measure of unemployment that is calculated by totalling the amount of people receiving unemployment-related benefits e.g. the number of people on job seeker's allowance (JSA)

International Labour Organisation (ILO) – A member organisation of the United Nations (UN) that collects statistics on labour market conditions and seeks to improve working conditions

Labour Force Survey (LFS) – A measure of unemployment based on a survey using the ILO definition of unemployment NOTE – ILO Definition of Unemployment: 1. Without a job, want a job, have actively sought work in the last four weeks and are available to start work in the next two weeks OR 2. Out of work, have found a job and are waiting to start it in the next two weeks

ILO Unemployment Rate – A measure of the percentage of the labour force who are without jobs, but are available to work, are willing to work and are looking for work

LFS (Advantages) / Claimant Count (Disadvantages):

- **Accuracy** – The LFS measure is thought to capture more of those who are unemployed. This is because some people are actively seeking work but are not entitled to claim benefits e.g. people whose partner is working or claiming benefits, and young people who are looking for work. These people would not appear in the claimant count
- **International Comparisons** – The LFS measure is widely used by most countries so it allows for better international comparisons. This is unlike the claimant count which is not suitable for such comparisons as the categories of people entitled to benefits differs from country to country
- **Benefit Fraud isn't Included** – The claimant count can be skewed as there may be fraudsters claiming benefits under false pretences

LFS (Disadvantages) / Claimant Count (Advantages):

- **Costly, Slow and Error-Prone** – The LFS measure is a lot more expensive to collect, and there is also a risk that it may be subject to sampling errors. The claimant count is also much quicker to compile than the LFS

Frictional Unemployment – Unemployment that occurs when someone is between jobs due to the inevitable time delays involved in job searching NOTE – This often occurs when someone is in search of a better potential job

Structural Unemployment – Unemployment that occurs as a result of changes in the pattern of economic activity. It is caused by geographical and/or occupational immobility

Geographical Immobility – Barriers to the movement of workers between areas NOTE – This may be due to high living costs (in the area where the jobs are), poor transport, poor information about jobs in different areas, or family ties. This results in regional mismatches, whereby unemployed workers are resident in particular regions of a country even though job vacancies exist elsewhere

Occupational Immobility – Barriers to workers changing occupation NOTE – This is likely due to a worker's skills no longer being needed anymore due to their industry closing down (e.g. the VHS industry), and so now they do not have the skills required for modern jobs. It may also simply be that an individual never bothered to get any skills or qualifications in the first place, and so the very low ones that they do have are not in demand from employers. This leads to skills mismatches, whereby workers are unemployed simply due to the fact that they do not possess the necessary skills and/or qualifications to fill existing job vacancies

Cyclical Unemployment – Unemployment that arises during the slowdown or recession phases of the economic cycle NOTE – The economic cycle will be explained in chapter 7.1

Demand-Deficient Unemployment – Unemployment that arises because of a deficiency of aggregate (total) demand in the economy, so there are simply not enough jobs available NOTE – This is sometimes known as cyclical unemployment as low aggregate demand always occurs in tandem with slowdowns and recessions. When demand, on the whole, in an economy is low, this means that the output firms will need to produce will decrease. Remember that labour is a derived demand, wanted not for its own sake, but for the level of output it can produce and what that output can be sold for. Lower output leads to a lower need for workers, resulting in unemployment as firms lay workers off

Classical Unemployment – When real wages are stuck above equilibrium level, resulting in a surplus of labour supplied e.g. NMWs and/or trade unions can cause this NOTE – This is sometimes known as excess real wage unemployment as it is caused by real wage inflexibility (real wages not falling down to equilibrium)

Seasonal Unemployment – Unemployment that occurs as a result of people working in industries that are not demanded all year round e.g. Santa Clauses being unemployed in the summer

Voluntary Unemployment – Unemployment that occurs when an individual chooses not to accept a job at the going wage rate NOTE – This could be because unemployment benefits may be so high that there is little incentive to bother getting a job. This could be worsened if income tax is very high

Involuntary Unemployment – Unemployment that occurs when an individual who would like to accept a job, at the going wage rate, is unable to find employment **NOTE – Demand deficient unemployment can be considered to be involuntary unemployment, as it occurs simply due to the fact that there is not enough jobs available in the economy**

Hysteresis – Unemployment causing unemployment

Long-Term Unemployment – Unemployment lasting for more than a year

BOTS CH (Costs of Unemployment):

B – Increased Spending on Benefits **–** If unemployment rises, the government will have to spend more on unemployment related benefits. This may mean that it has to reduce spending on other essential services (such as education and health) or will have to raise its borrowing or tax rates. Effectively, this means that the money spent on benefits will have opportunity cost, both in terms of the forgone spending on essential services and also the forgone potential growth rates in the future which may be limited by high tax rates

O – Lost Output **–** Having people, who are willing and able to work, without jobs is a waste of resources. If these people were in work, the country would produce more goods and services and so material living standards would be higher

T – Lost Tax **Revenue –** If more people were in work, incomes, spending and possibly profits would be higher. This would mean that the government would collect more tax revenue from all forms of taxes (income, expenditure and corporation tax) and this revenue could be spent on education, health, transport etc... which could improve the quality of people's lives and increase the country's productive capacity

S – Pressure on Other Forms of Government Spending **–** When people are unemployed, they are more likely to suffer health problems (including mental health problems), marital difficulties and some even turn to crime. More health problems mean longer waiting lists for healthcare if the government don't increase their spending on the health sector or raise its productivity. Marital break-ups increase the need for housing benefit and the provision of social housing. Increased crime means that the government have to spend more on police and the judicial system

C – Costs **to the Unemployed –** The following are potential costs to those who are unemployed:

- Poor health
- Family break-ups
- Unemployment benefit will likely be lower than the previous income that the person had
- Some people feel a loss of self-purpose, worth or status when becoming unemployed
- The children tend to have worse health
- The children tend to do worse at school due to having less educational tools at home, a lower chance of having their own room to study in, and their parents tend to have lower expectations of them which can cause demotivation

H – Hysteresis **–** The longer people are out of work, the more difficult it is for them to get employed, which, if long term enough, can reduce the productive capacity of the economy. Employers are less reluctant to hire someone who has been out of work for a long time because:

1. Being out of a job that long may suggest that they are not good workers

2. The longer someone is unemployed, the more their skills deteriorate and the more out of touch they become with advances in working methods and technology

On the supply side, the long term unemployed tend to seek work less actively over time because:

1. They may lose their work ethic and get used to being at home
2. They may become discouraged by the continuous rejections

Full Employment – Occurs when people who are economically active and also willing and able to work (at going wage rates) are able to find employment NOTE – This doesn't include workers who are changing between jobs (frictionally unemployed) as there will always be movement of workers and lag time in an economy. Additionally, we often don't include structural unemployment as such people are either not willing or not able to work. Lastly, we don't include voluntary unemployment as such people are simply unwilling to work. This means that full employment does not necessarily mean that there is no unemployment. There will be some arbitrary number picked by the government (such as 5%) that will represent the amount of unemployment expected to take place when there is 'full' employment

5.1 AGGREGATE DEMAND

Aggregate Demand (AD) – The total demand for a country's finished goods and services at a given price level in a given time period NOTE – It shows planned expenditure at any given price level

Aggregate Demand (AD) Formula – $C + I + G + (X - M)$ NOTE – As AD is planned expenditure at any given price level, AD is essentially the same as the total expenditure of an economy. We know that the total expenditure formula is $C + I + G + (X - M)$, and so it can be seen that calculating AD and calculating nominal GDP, is the same (i.e. they use the same formula)

Real GDP = Real Output = Real Income = Real Expenditure NOTE – Some people even call them national output, national income or national expenditure, but I prefer to use the word 'real'

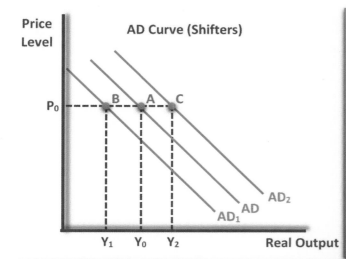

First of all, notice that the y-axis has been labelled 'Price Level' NOT 'Price', and also that the x-axis has been labelled 'Real Output' NOT 'Quantity', with point labels using the letter Y rather than Q (Edexcel may actually deduct marks if you use Q instead of Y). You could actually label the x-axis quite a few other terms such as real GDP or real income, however, I prefer to use real output as it links most smoothly with labour being a derived demand. Now, AD basically shifts when there is a change in any of its components. Let's say that, for example, consumption fell due to a rise in income tax. This would mean that AD would be lower at any given price level, resulting in AD decreasing from AD to AD_1. This would cause real output to fall from Y_0 to Y_1 with the price level remaining at P_0.

Suppose that instead government spending rose as a result of increased government spending on education. This would mean that AD would be higher at any given price level, resulting in AD increasing from AD to AD_2. This would cause real output to rise from Y_0 to Y_2 with the price level remaining at P_0. Bear in mind, also, that changes in real output represent changes in short run economic growth.

Why the AD Curve is Downwards Sloping:

- There are 3 reasons as to why the AD curve is thought to be downwards sloping:
  - The wealth effect
  - The interest rate effect
  - The international trade effect
- **The wealth effect:**
  - A fall in the price level will mean that deflation has occurred. Assuming nominal income to be fixed, this will mean that real disposable income has increased due to the fact that deflation means that the purchasing power of money has increased. As a result, you are now wealthier and so are more likely to increase your spending on goods and services (as you have a greater ability to do so), resulting in real expenditure increasing
- **The interest rate effect:**
  - A fall in the price level means that deflation is occurring. Governments (and central banks) don't like deflation and will want to do their best to try and

stimulate economic activity. As a result, they will lower interest rates in a bid to increase consumption and investment, and so this leads to a rise in real output (or real expenditure, they are the same anyway)

- **The international trade effect:**
  - As the price level of a country falls, this means that the goods made in said country (some of which will later be exported) will likely, on average, fall in price. Ceteris paribus, this will likely lead to exports becoming more price competitive (cheaper) than imports, resulting in increased spending on exports (from foreigners, an injection) and decreased spending on imports (from domestic consumers, a leakage). As a result, real expenditure should rise

Wealth – A stock of assets that have financial value e.g. property, shares, bank deposits

Income – A flow of money earned over a period of time e.g. wages, salaries etc...

Consumer Confidence – How optimistic consumers are about future economic prospects

Transfer Payments – Money transferred from one individual, or group, to another, not in return for any goods or services e.g. state benefits

Disposable Income – Income after taxes on income have been deducted and state benefits have been added NOTE – This is effectively the money that consumers have available for consumption or saving

Interest Rates – The charge for borrowing money and the amount paid for lending money (or saving) NOTE – A very simplified explanation of this would be that if interest rates were 2%, that would mean that if you borrowed £100 from the bank, you would have to pay back £102 to the bank, and if you saved £100 in the bank, the bank would pay you back £102. What this essentially means, is that lower interest rates incentivise you to borrow because it is cheaper to do so, and higher interest rates incentivise you to save because there is potential to make a higher return on your money

WIBI CUT (Consumption Determinants):

W – Wealth – If the amount and/or value of wealth people have increases, this means that people will be more able to spend on products (you can borrow money against your house, for example) and are also more likely to be willing to do so as consumer confidence would likely rise. Both effects would likely lead to consumption increasing

I – Interest Rates – If interest rates fall, this means that people will get less returns on their savings and that it will be cheaper for people to borrow. Reduced incentive to save, combined with increased incentive to borrow, is likely to increase spending on goods and services, meaning that consumption will rise

B – Benefits – If government spending on unemployment benefits increases, this will lead to a rise in the disposable income of those who are unemployed. Those who are unemployed (and also low-income earners in general) tend to have a high marginal propensity to consume (MPC), meaning that when given additional money they are likely to spend a very large proportion of it. As a result, spending on goods and services will likely rise thus leading to higher consumption

I – Inflation – If inflation is very high and people expect prices to rise by a lot in the future, they may decide to increase their spending now which would lead to an increase in their current consumption

C – Consumer Confidence – If consumer confidence increases for any reason (e.g. high economic growth figure is published, average incomes are rising fast etc…) this can boost the level of consumption

U – Unemployment – A decrease in the level of unemployment likely means that more people are employed. More people in employment means that more people have incomes with which they can spend on goods and services, and so this is likely to increase consumption

T – Income Tax – If income tax falls, this will lead to an increase in disposable income for a majority of the population, which will likely lead to increased spending on goods and services and thus consumption

NOTE – As you can see, just about anything that increases people's disposable income is likely to lead to an increase in consumption, as their ability to purchase goods and services would have increased. Also note that anything that directly influences the level of saving is also likely to have an effect on consumption

Consumption Function – The functional relationship between consumption and disposable income; its position depends upon other non-income factors (i.e. wealth, interest rates etc…) that affect how much households spend on consumption

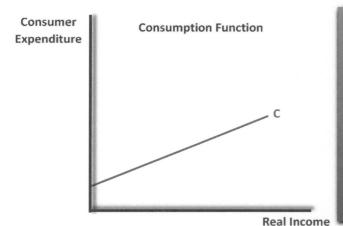

This basic function simply shows that as real income rises, so does consumption / consumer expenditure. Other determinants such as wealth and interest rates are thought to shift the consumption curve. It should also be noted that the marginal propensity to consume (MPC) is the slope / gradient of the curve (MPC will be talked more about later). An additional point, is that where the consumption function hits the y-axis is known as autonomous consumption. This is the idea that even with no income, people will still find a way to buy essentials like food so that they can eat. This will likely either be by borrowing or running down savings.

Corporation Tax – A tax on a firm's profits

Retained Profits – Profits kept by firms to finance investment or debt

Business Confidence – How optimistic firms are about future economic prospects

TIP SPIT CC (Investment Determinants):

T – Advances in Technology – A firm may buy new capital equipment if it thinks that it will produce better quality products or produce products more cheaply. In either case, the firm would expect to earn higher profits. In the first case it would be because the firm would anticipate higher demand, and in the second case it would be because the firm would anticipate that its average cost of production would fall. Additionally, if other firms are investing in more new technology, then a firm may be forced to do so as well in order to stay competitive and maintain profit levels

I – Interest Rates – A rise in interest rates, for example, could decrease investment due to the following reasons:

1. Higher interest rates will increase the opportunity cost of investment. This is because if a firm chooses to invest, they forgo the potential returns they could be making by placing their retained profits in a bank
2. Whilst a lot of investment comes from retained profits, some of it is done through borrowing, which would now be more expensive
3. Firms will likely anticipate consumer spending falling because consumers are less likely to borrow and more likely to save. Firms won't want to invest in the face of falling demand
4. Firms may lose out on potential investors that would have provided further funds for investment. This would be because some potential investors may decide to just put their money in savings accounts as the return for savings is now higher

P – Price of Capital – Ceteris paribus, a reduction in the price of capital will lead to an increase in investment, and an increase in the price of capital will lead to a reduction in investment

S – Subsidies – An increase in subsidies to firms effectively reduces the costs of production for said firms, which in turn increases their level of retained profits. This means that they have more funds available for investment which will likely lead to investment increasing **NOTE – Another way of thinking about it would be the firm simply adding the subsidy straight onto their profits. Arguably, however, the more fully fledged explanation is to talk about their cost of production effectively being reduced**

P – Profits – A rise in profits (for any reason) is likely to increase a firm's ability to invest, and also likely to make a firm more willing to invest due to being more optimistic about the future. Both effects are likely to increase investment

I – Real Disposable Income – If real disposable income rises, then demand for consumer goods and services is also likely to rise. This means that firms will likely need to expand and will likely need to do so through investment (assuming they were previously operating at full capacity) **NOTE – Consumption and investment are linked in the sense that rises in consumption can technically lead to increases in investment**

T – Corporation Tax – An increase in corporation tax, for example, decreases the amount of profits that firms can retain and use for investment, and so this would likely reduce investment

C – Spare Capacity – Firms are more likely to invest when they are operating at, or close to, full capacity, because with spare capacity it may be possible to increase output without investment

C – Business Confidence – If firms feel more optimistic about future economic prospects, they are more likely to increase investment

NOTE – Consumption is thought to typically be the largest component of AD, and investment is thought to be the most volatile

FEET (Government Spending Determinants):

F – Government's View on the Extent of Market Failure and its Ability to Correct it – In countries where there is a high level of state intervention, government spending usually forms a larger proportion of AD than in countries where free market forces play a more dominant role

E – The Level of Economic Activity – If there is high levels of unemployment, a government may raise spending (on anything) to increase AD and thus the real output of the economy. On the other hand, if there is a very high inflation rate, a government may instead reduce its spending

E – Election Cycles – Voters can put pressure on the government to increase spending, and equally a government may also decide to increase spending, just before a general election, in order to gain votes

T – The Threat of Social Collapse – The threat of war, terrorism or rising crime may lead to the government increasing spending on police and/or the military

X – M = Net Exports (NX) = Net Trade = Trade Balance NOTE – A lot of this time we have been calling X and M, exports and imports, which is true to some extent, but it's worth clarifying on what is actually going on. X or exports is really export revenue (the value of exports) and M or imports is really import expenditure (the value of imports). For now, this won't be of great importance, but later we will learn about how the PED of imports and/or exports can affect this. So from here onwards, I will mostly be using the terminology of export revenue and import expenditure

Tariff – A tax on imports

IRI PIE (Net Exports (X-M) Determinants):

I – Inflation – If UK inflation, for example, was increasing at a rate faster than that of our major trading partners, this would likely make our exports less price competitive (as they would, on average, be rising in price), and the imports of our major trading partners more price competitive. The resulting effect would likely be a fall in export revenue and a rise in import expenditure

R – Government Restrictions on Free Trade – If a country (let's say country A) removes a trade restriction, such as a tariff, this will likely lead to an increase in import expenditure in country A, as imports would now be cheaper without the tax. If another foreign country (let's say country B) removed tariffs on its imports, which happens to include country A's exports, this will likely lead to an increase in export revenue for country A as their exports will now be cheaper in country B

I – Real Disposable Income at Home or Abroad – If real disposable incomes are falling at home (country A), possibly due to a recession at home, this may lead to an increase in export revenue as domestic firms attempt to compete harder in international markets, rather than at home due to the low levels of domestic consumption (caused by the falling incomes). Additionally, the low levels of domestic consumption may lead to lower import expenditure as consumers will have less disposable income to spend on imports. If a foreign country (country B) experiences falling real disposable income (due to a recession as well), and happens to be a major trading partner to country A, their fall in import expenditure means that country A's export revenue will fall (Country A's exports are Country B's imports). The opposite would of course occur if real disposable incomes were rising in either of the countries

P – Productivity – A general rise in productivity in the UK, for example, is likely to lower average costs of production for many firms, meaning that they will be able to supply more products, many of which will be exports, at lower prices. This increase in price competitiveness of UK exports and reduction in price competitiveness of imports is likely to lead to an increase in export revenue and a reduction in import expenditure

I – Innovation – A rise in innovation (and thus technology) is likely to increase the quality of exports. This should cause the demand curve for exports to increase due to their increased quality competitiveness, relative to imports, resulting in an increase in export revenue and a fall in import expenditure

E – Exchange Rates – If a country's exchange rate rises, for example, this will lead to the country's imports becoming cheaper and its exports becoming more expensive. This means that the imports have become more price competitive whilst the exports have become less price competitive, and so there would likely be a rise in import expenditure and a fall in export revenue **NOTE – If the £:$ exchange rate increased from £1:$1 to £1:$2, you can see that for the same amount of money (£1) a UK citizen is getting more dollars and thus will find it cheaper to buy American imports now. For a US citizen, they will now need to pay more dollars ($2, rather than $1) for the same amount of pounds (£1), and so they will now find it more expensive to buy UK exports**

Multiplier Effect – The process by which any change in a component of AD results in a greater final change in real GDP **NOTE – The multiplier ratio is known as the ratio of a change in equilibrium real output (the after effect) to the autonomous change that brought it about (the initial change)**

Marginal Propensity to Consume (MPC) – The proportion of additional income that is spent on the consumption of goods and services **NOTE – This can be looked at for individuals or entire economies (and the same is true for the upcoming terms). For individuals, we would say that those who are poor tend to have a high MPC compared to wealthier people who are, on the contrary, thought to have a higher MPS (and thus low MPC) due to the idea that they are more likely to have satisfied most of their consumption needs. For an economy, it would be a general trend. For those of us in the UK, for example, we generally have a very high MPC, whereas those living in Japan tend to have a low MPC, and instead tend to have a high MPS**

Marginal Propensity to Consume (MPC) Formula – $\frac{change\ in\ consumption}{change\ in\ income}$ **NOTE – This will either be the income of an individual or of the entire economy (national income). The same thinking is relevant to the upcoming terms as well. Additionally, all changes on the top of the fraction (for all of these terms) is in money terms e.g. change in consumption = £20bn (for the UK)**

Marginal Propensity to Save (MPS) – The proportion of additional income that is saved

Marginal Propensity to Save (MPS) Formula – $\frac{change\ in\ savings}{change\ in\ income}$

Marginal Propensity to Tax (MPT) – The proportion of additional income that is taxed

Marginal Propensity to Tax (MPT) Formula – $\frac{change\ in\ taxes}{change\ in\ income}$

Marginal Propensity to Import (MPI) – The proportion of additional income that is spent on imports

Marginal Propensity to Import (MPI) Formula – $\dfrac{change\ in\ imports}{change\ in\ income}$

Marginal Propensity to Withdraw (MPW) – The proportion of additional income that leaks (is withdrawn) from the circular flow of income **NOTE – It is basically all of the leakages from the circular flow of income**

Marginal Propensity to Withdraw (MPW) Formula – $MPS + MPT + MPI$

Multiplier Formula(s) – $k = \dfrac{1}{MPW}$ OR $k = \dfrac{1}{1-MPC}$ **NOTE – the multiplier is called 'k' in this**

Multiplier Example:

- If $k = \dfrac{1}{MPW} = \dfrac{1}{0.5} = 2$ this means that the size of the multiplier is 2, and also that half of any increase in national income leaks out of the circular flow because MPW is $0.5 = \dfrac{1}{2}$

- This means that if £5 billion where injected into the economy, £2.5 billion would leak out but the other £2.5 billion would go back around, and then of that £2.5 billion (that has gone back around), £1.25 billion would leak out, and so on

- You would get £8.75 billion (the initial £5 billion + £2.5 billion + £1.25 billion) and this would continue until national income increased by a total of £10 billion (twice as big as the initial injection of £5 billion, which makes sense as the multiplier was 2)

- A positive multiplier effect can be explained verbally as well. If there was a rise in national income due to a new housing project from the government, for example, this would lead to an increase in factor incomes, particularly in the form of wages (for the labour employed) and rent (for the land used). How much of this stays in the economy and how much of it leaks out basically determines the size of the multiplier, and so leads to the effects talked about previously

- You can also get negative multiplier effects as well. This would be when an initial decrease in an injection (or an increase in a leakage) leads to a greater final decrease in real GDP, the opposite of a positive one essentially

- Let's say AD decreased due to a decrease in export revenue, leading to real output falling. This fall in real output would likely lead to firms laying off workers as labour is a derived demand. This now means, however, that there are more people who are unemployed and on benefits (getting a lot less money than they used to), leading to lower consumption, lower AD and so on

AD Curve (Multiplier)

The multiplier effect can be shown on a graph with AD simply shifting two times. It first may increase from AD to AD_1, due to an increase in investment, causing real output to increase from Y_0 to Y_1. The multiplier effect, however, may cause AD to increase from AD_1 to AD_2, causing real output to increase from Y_1 to Y_2. You can see that the initial change in the component of AD, investment, has led to a greater final change in real output. When we draw AD diagrams, however, we just skip the curve in the middle (AD_1), and so you could just say (in writing) that your diagram assumes a multiplier effect (if you want to).

5.2 AGGREGATE SUPPLY

Aggregate Supply (AS) – The total amount that producers in an economy are willing and able to supply at a given price level in a given time period NOTE – This will either be short run or long run AS

Short Run – The time period when at least one factor of production, usually capital, is fixed in quantity e.g. a firm does not have time to sell off its existing building, end a renting contract, extend an existing building or acquire a new building in the short run

Short Run Aggregate Supply (SRAS) – Shows the total level of production available in an economy at a given price level, assuming labour costs and other input prices to be fixed

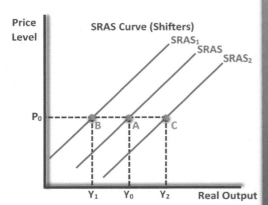

As stated in the definition, labour costs (e.g. nominal wages) and other input prices (e.g. oil prices) are fixed. Wages may be 'sticky' due to workers being slow to realise that prices are increasing, and so they don't bargain for higher wages, plus a lot of them may also be stuck on contracts. Firms' contracts with raw material suppliers may also be agreed in such a way that firms agree to pay a fixed price for resources in the short run. This effectively means that this curve assumes that a firm's costs of production are mostly fixed in the short run, meaning that an increase in the price level suggests that firms can earn higher profits ($Profit = Total\ Revenue\ (PxQ) - Total\ Costs$) as prices are increasing. The increased profitability gives firms the incentive to increase their production / output, leading to an upwards sloping SRAS curve.

As costs of production are assumed to be fixed in the short run, this means that a change in costs of production will mean that the curve would need to be drawn in a different position (shifted). If costs of production (for most firms) rose, this would cause SRAS to decrease from SRAS to SRAS$_1$, resulting in real output falling from Y$_0$ to Y$_1$. If, on the other hand, costs of production (for most firms) fell, this would cause SRAS to increase from SRAS to SRAS$_2$, resulting in real output increasing from Y$_0$ to Y$_2$.

RT RW (SRAS Shifters / Determinants):

R – Resource Costs – If a common resource input, such as oil, rose in price, this would cause a lot of firms' costs of production to increase, resulting in SRAS decreasing. This is because oil prices indirectly affect transportation, energy and even direct production costs (e.g. plastic producers need oil to make plastic, and some firms need plastic for packaging) of many firms in the economy NOTE – Exchange rate fluctuations can also change resource costs as well. Many suppliers use imported raw materials (such as oil) and, of course, changes in exchange rates can change the prices of all imports. This means that a fall in the exchange rate, for example, would make imported raw material prices higher (as a lower exchange rate makes exports cheaper and imports more expensive), thus causing costs of production for a large amount of firms to rise, further causing SRAS to shift left. The opposite would of course occur if the exchange rate rose

T – Tax – If corporation tax increases, this will effectively increase the costs of production of all firms in an economy by taking a larger chunk out of their profits and reducing their profit margins, causing SRAS to decrease NOTE – An increase in indirect tax could also have a similar effect

R – Regulations – If a government begins to start enforcing large amounts of regulations (e.g. environmental laws) on lots of firms in an economy, this is likely to lead to an increase in the costs of production for a lot of firms, thus resulting in SRAS decreasing

W – Wages – If wages for a majority of firms rose (e.g. NMW was implemented or increased), this would cause a lot of firms' costs of production to increase, resulting in SRAS decreasing

Long Run – The time period when the quantities of all factors of production are variable

Long Run Aggregate Supply (LRAS) – Shows the relationship between the total supply of products and the price level in the long run

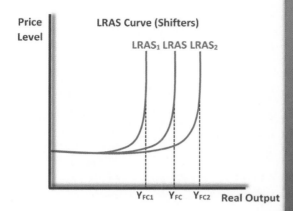

The LRAS curve can be broken down into three different parts (looking at one curve). The first part of the LRAS curve is perfectly elastic (horizontal), which means that increases in real output across that part of the curve result in no changes in the price level. This occurs due to the fact that at the start of an LRAS curve there are many unemployed (unused) factors of production. This means that firms are able to expand production as demand increases, without seeing any great rise in costs, as competition for resources is low due to the vast amount of them. The second part of the LRAS curve begins to curve upwards, which means that increases in real output across this part of the curve result in the price level increasing. This is due to the fact that resources are becoming scarcer and so cost-push inflation is beginning to arise, due to the fact that the high competition (from firms) for resources is resulting in their prices being bid up.

The last part of the LRAS curve is perfectly inelastic (vertical), which means that real output simply can't increase any further, and so the economy has reached full capacity or full employment (I prefer to call it full capacity, but just pick what you prefer). At this point, all resources are fully employed and it is simply no longer possible for firms to increase production. Shifts in LRAS are caused by changes in the productive capacity (or productive potential, either term is fine) of the economy. The specific factors affecting this will be discussed on the next page. If the productive potential of the economy was to decrease, this would result in LRAS decreasing from LRAS to $LRAS_1$, causing the maximum level of real output to decrease from Y_{FC} to Y_{FC1}. If the productive potential of the economy was to increase, this would result in LRAS increasing from LRAS to $LRAS_2$, causing the maximum level of real output to increase from Y_{FC} to Y_{FC2}. Bear in mind, also, that changes in Y_{FC} (which can be written as Y_{FE}, if you prefer to say full employment) represent changes in long run economic growth.

Productivity – Output of a good or service, per factor of production, per period of time; the efficiency of a factor of production

Labour Productivity – Output per worker, per period of time

Human Capital – The stock of knowledge, skills and expertise that contribute to a worker's productivity

Capital Productivity – Output per unit of capital, per period of time

Depreciation – A gradual decrease in the value of the physical capital stock, over time, as it is subject to wear and tear

Net Investment – Gross (total) investment minus depreciation

CELL (LRAS Shifters / Determinants):

C – Quantity or Quality of Capital – If the quantity of capital increases due to an increase in net investment (which could be caused by any of its determinants), for example, this will lead to an increase in the capital stock. A larger capital stock will increase the productive potential of the economy (more capital goods that can be used to increase output) and so cause LRAS to increase. If the quality of capital increased (via improved technology) as a result of increased spending by firms or the government on R&D, for example, this would also increase the productive potential of the economy (it would likely increase capital productivity, meaning that more goods and services could be produced in the same time period), and so also cause LRAS to increase NOTE – Poor or insufficient investment could result in net investment falling, if depreciation isn't being taken care of. This would, of course, reduce the size of the capital stock. It can also be argued that increases in investment can lead to increases in both the quantity and quality of the capital stock. This is because when firms carry out investment, the new capital they buy may come with new technology. This argument, however, is not typically used by students

E – Quantity or Quality of Entrepreneurship – The quantity of entrepreneurship could increase if the government, for example, reduced rules and regulations placed on firms, increased privatisation (e.g. returned the provision of health services back to the private sector) or provided more incentives for people to start businesses (e.g. lower corporation tax). This would increase the productive potential of the economy (because entrepreneurs are likely to be able to organise and use resources in a more efficient manner, allowing more output to be produced from the same amount of resources) and so cause LRAS to increase. The quality of entrepreneurship could be increased by higher levels of management training, and increased provision and reform of education. This would, of course, also increase the productive potential of the economy and so also increase LRAS

L – Quantity or Quality of Labour – The quantity of labour (specifically, people in the labour force) could increase due to higher immigration, higher retirement age (meaning that more people would be obliged to work before they could retire and live off of a pension) or more women (who may have been looking after their home) deciding to enter the labour force. This would increase the productive potential of the economy (more labour to create goods and services) causing LRAS to increase. The quality of labour could be improved by increased government spending on education and training, for example. This would also increase the productive potential of the economy (increased human capital would increase labour productivity, meaning that more goods and services could be produced in the same time period) and so also cause LRAS to increase

L – Quantity or Quality of Land – The quantity of land could increase via land reclamation (the restoration of previously unusable or damaged land) or through the discovery of natural resources. This would increase the productive potential of the economy (more natural resources to use for production) and so cause LRAS to increase NOTE – I can't personally think of any ways that the 'quality' of land could be increased. If you manage to think of any specific ways that the quality of land could be increased, then feel free to use them, however, if you are in an exam, I would probably play it safe and focus mostly on capital or labour as LRAS shifters (if given the choice)

Double Shifters:

- You may or may not have noticed this, but it is indeed possible that changes in certain factors can result in what I would call 'double shifters' (not a real term), whereby both AD and LRAS would increase at the same time. Below are some of the main ones:
    - **Net Investment** – An increase in net investment, for example, would increase both AD (because investment is a component of AD) and LRAS (because the capital stock would increase in size)
    - **Government Spending** – Government spending on education and training, health, or infrastructure are the main ones. As stated before, spending on education and training can increase the human capital of those in the labour force. Improved health services mean that people shouldn't be off work sick for so long (shorter waiting lists) and people's general health may even improve, resulting in an increase in productivity of a large number of workers. Infrastructure projects can improve transport conditions, making it cheaper and more efficient for firms to use supplier vehicles, and also easier for people to travel to schools, hospitals and to work in more distant places (which can further increase productivity). The previous reasons explain why government spending can increase productive potential (and thus LRAS), but they also increase AD as government spending is a component of AD
    - **Size of Labour Force** – Anything that increases the size of the labour force will result in the productive potential of the economy increasing (and thus LRAS). AD, however, can also increase as more people in the labour force means more people earning disposable income (or people earning higher disposable income), and thus higher consumption which can increase AD (as consumption is a component of AD)
- NOTE – What these double shifters would look like on a graph will be shown on a later page

Classical / Monetarist Economists – Economists who believed that the macroeconomy always adjusts back to the full employment level of output NOTE – They drew LRAS as a vertical curve

Natural Rate of Output – Another term used by classical economists for describing the full employment level

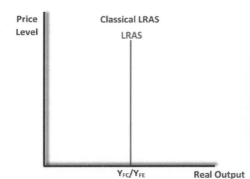

I don't believe that you need to know very much about this model, but the diagram on the left shows what classical economists thought the LRAS curve looked like. They believed that, in the long run, everything would adjust, resulting in real output being equal to full employment / capacity.

Keynesian Economists – Economists who believed that the macroeconomy could settle at an equilibrium level that was lower than full employment / capacity NOTE – This is the curved LRAS we were drawing earlier

5.3 MACROECONOMIC EQUILIBRIUM

Macroeconomic Equilibrium – A state of economic activity where aggregate demand equals aggregate supply and real GDP is not changing

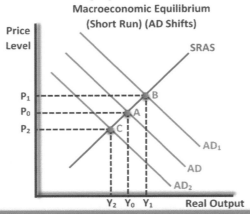

Macroeconomic Equilibrium (Short Run) (AD Shifts)

The two diagrams on this page show macroeconomic equilibrium occurring in the short run. The above graph starts with AD being equal to SRAS, resulting in a price level of P_0 at level of real output Y_0. An increase in AD from AD to AD_1, results in the price level increasing from P_0 to P_1 with real output increasing from Y_0 to Y_1. A decrease in AD from AD to AD_2, results in the price level decreasing from P_0 to P_2 with real output decreasing from Y_0 to Y_2. Hence, it can be deduced that, with both AD and SRAS present, an increase in AD will have an upward pressure on the price level and an upward pressure on real output, whilst a decrease in AD will have a downward pressure on the price level and a downward pressure on real output.

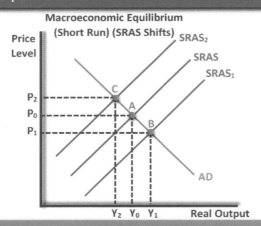

Macroeconomic Equilibrium (Short Run) (SRAS Shifts)

This diagram also starts with AD being equal to SRAS, resulting in a price level of P_0 at level of real output Y_0. An increase in SRAS from SRAS to $SRAS_1$, results in the price level decreasing from P_0 to P_1 with real output increasing from Y_0 to Y_1. A decrease in SRAS from SRAS to $SRAS_2$, results in the price level increasing from P_0 to P_2 with real output decreasing from Y_0 to Y_2. Hence, it can be deduced that, with both AD and SRAS present, an increase in SRAS will have a downward pressure on the price level and an upward pressure on real output, whilst a decrease in SRAS will have an upward pressure on the price level and a downward pressure on real output. If both curves (AD and SRAS) were to shift at once, we would see that there would be opposing pressures on price, and possibly real output, and so the final outcome would depend on the extent of the changes in AD and SRAS.

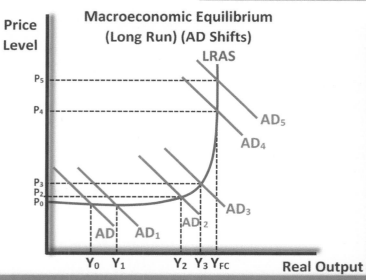

The diagram on the left shows how the effects of AD shifts differ depending on what part of the LRAS curve it is on. An increase in AD from AD to AD_1, results in an increase in real output from Y_0 to Y_1 with no change in the price level (that remains at P_0). This shows that AD shifts on the bottom part of the LRAS curve, only cause changes in real output but have no effect on the price level. Next, an increase in AD from AD_2 to AD_3, results in real output increasing from Y_2 to Y_3 with the price level increasing from P_2 to P_3. This shows that AD shifts on the middle, curved part of the LRAS curve, cause changes in both real output and the price level.

Lastly, an increase in AD from AD_4 to AD_5, results in no change in real output (which remains at Y_{FC}) with the price level increasing from P_4 to P_5. This shows that AD shifts on the top part of the LRAS curve have no effect on real output and are purely inflationary. This essentially means that increases in AD can still lead to increases in nominal output (GDP), but any increase in nominal output has been caused purely by price rises (this is because the economy is at full capacity, and so it's not possible for production to rise). As a result, once it is converted to real output (GDP), the real output figure remains exactly the same, as the inflation is deducted from the nominal GDP figure.

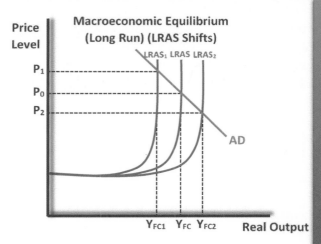

The diagram on the left shows the effects of LRAS shifts on the price level and real output. The diagram starts with AD equal to LRAS where, in this case, AD is operating at the level that produces the maximum level of real output (Y_{FC}) at a price level of P_0. A decrease in LRAS from LRAS to $LRAS_1$, causes real output to fall from Y_{FC} to Y_{FC1} and the price level to increase from P_0 to P_1. An increase in LRAS from LRAS to $LRAS_2$ causes real output to rise from Y_{FC} to Y_{FC2} and the price level to decrease from P_0 to P_2. Hence, it can be deduced that, with both AD and LRAS present, an increase in LRAS will have a downward pressure on the price level and an upward pressure on real output (if AD is high enough), whilst a decrease in LRAS will have an upward pressure on the price level and a downward pressure on real output (if AD is high enough).

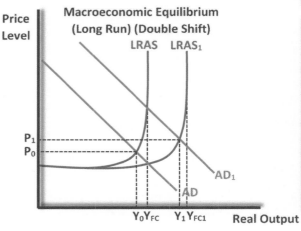

The diagram on the left simply shows the effects of a 'double shift'. Starting where AD equals LRAS, results in real output of Y_0 at a price level of P_0. An increase in AD from AD to AD_1, combined with an increase in LRAS from LRAS to $LRAS_1$, results in real output increasing from Y_0 to Y_1, the price level increasing from P_0 to P_1 and the productive potential of the economy increasing from Y_{FC} to Y_{FC1}. You will see that, even on this diagram, trying to include Y_{FC} begins to make the diagram somewhat cramped. On the following page, I will talk about the three potential options you have to deal with this.

The first option is that you draw the diagram so big that it avoids the risk of the examiner not being able to read your diagram. If the first option seems like too much of a risk, or makes the diagram more cramped than you would like, then you have the option of drawing AD so high on the LRAS curves that the real output values are equal to the Y_{FC} values (like on the 'LRAS Shifts' diagram on the previous page). The last option is to simply not write the Y_{FC} stuff in, but instead just talk about it verbally (I believe this is what most people do).

AD/AS Diagram Analysis:

- You need to be able to talk about how changes on your AD/AS diagram affect the key macroeconomic performance indicators. The points you can talk about are below:
    - **Economic Growth** – Changes in real output lead to either rises or falls in short run economic growth. Changes in LRAS and thus Y_{FC}, that have been caused by changes in productive potential, represent either rises or falls in long run economic growth
    - **Employment** – If there is an increase in real output, this will likely lead to a rise in employment due to the fact that labour is a derived demand, wanted not for its own sake, but for the level of output it can produce and what that output can be sold for. As a result, firms will want to hire more labour in order to increase output and maximise their profitability, resulting in employment rising. You would say the opposite if there was a decrease in real output
    - **Inflation** – Changes in the price level, caused by changes in AD, either show increases or decreases in demand-pull inflation. Changes in the price level, caused by changes in AS (SRAS or LRAS), either show increases or decreases in cost-push inflation. If inflation increases (on a LRAS diagram), you would say it's due to the fact that there is increased competition between firms for the remaining factors of production, either because AD has increased (which will increase the demand for resources as they are a derived demand), or because there are less resources available and/or the existing resources are being used less efficiently (this would occur if LRAS decreased). You would say the opposite if inflation decreased **NOTE – Decreased inflation will either lead to disinflation or deflation**
    - **Balance of Payments** – If inflation increases, this will likely lead to exports becoming less price competitive, resulting in lower export revenue and higher import expenditure, and thus a worsening of the balance of payments (this is explained in the next chapter). You would say the opposite if inflation decreased

AD/AS Diagram Evaluation:

- Analysis of AD/AS diagrams and their effects on the economy depend on the following:
    - Depends on the extent of the shifts in AD and/or SRAS/LRAS
    - Depends on the size of the multiplier effect (if AD has shifted)
    - Depends on the initial level of economic activity (where AD starts on the LRAS curve)
    - Assumes ceteris paribus e.g. another component of AD may have changed, which could change the final outcome

NOTE – There won't be any more AD/AS diagrams in this revision guide, and so I will simply talk about effects on AD and AS verbally. If, by any chance, you have forgotten how to draw them, just come back to this chapter

6.1 BALANCE OF PAYMENTS

Balance of Payments – A set of accounts showing the transactions carried out between residents of a country and the rest of the world; records money flows into and out of a country over a period of time **NOTE – It consists of a current account, a financial account and a capital account**

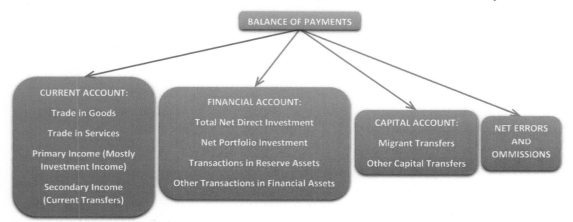

Above, is a diagram showing the components of the balance of payments. The definitions below will explain the components of each account (bear in mind that 'NET ERRORS AND OMMISSIONS' is not an 'account' it just adjusts the balance of payments to ensure that the final sum of all of the accounts equals 0). An important point to note is that it is most crucial you know the components of the current account (that's why it's in green), as it is the one you use most and it is also declared in the specification that you must be able to explain what each component is. It isn't specifically said that you need to be able to explain / define what the components of the financial and capital account are (although I think that knowing the explanations of them makes them easier to memorise), but you do need to know the names of the components and should also know the definitions of the financial account and the capital account. Below are definitions / brief explanations of all of the accounts and their components.

Current Account – An account identifying transactions in goods and services, primary income and secondary income (current transfers) between the residents of a country and the rest of the world **NOTE – A current account deficit is when the money leaving a country in terms of trade in goods and services, primary income and secondary income exceeds what enters the country in terms of trade in goods and services, primary income and secondary income. A current account surplus is simply the opposite**

Visible Trade – Trade in goods

Invisible Trade – Trade in services

Trade in Goods – Export revenue from goods minus import expenditure on goods

Trade in Services – Export revenue from services minus import expenditure on services

Trade Balance – The sum of trade in goods and trade in services

Trade Surplus – The value of exports (export revenue) exceeding the value of imports (import expenditure) **i.e. X-M is positive**

Trade Deficit – The value of imports (import expenditure) exceeding the value of exports (export revenue) **i.e. X-M is negative**

Primary Income – Compensation of employees, investment income and other primary income coming in from abroad minus compensation of employees, investment income and other primary income going abroad

Investment Income – The interest payments, dividends and profits coming from abroad to domestic investors minus the interest payments, dividends and profits going abroad to foreign investors **NOTE – If I bought a share in Microsoft and, over the years, I received dividends (money from the company to me, the shareholder), that would be a credit (a positive value) in investment income. If a foreigner put their money in a UK bank and received an interest payment from it as a result, that would be a debit (negative value) in investment income. The sum of these credits and debits gives the final value of investment income**

Current Transfers (Secondary Income) – Transfer payments entering the country minus transfer payments leaving the country **NOTE – This effectively consists of general government transfer payments (i.e. cash transfers between governments) and 'other sectors' transfer payments which includes things such as remittances (money sent back, by migrants, to extended family in their home country) and cash transfers for disaster relief. An additional point to note is that sometimes remittances go under compensation of employees (in primary income) depending on the length of the stay of the migrant and where they are working**

Income Balance – The sum of primary income and secondary income (current transfers)

Financial Account – An account identifying transactions, in the form of financial assets, between the residents of a country and the rest of the world

Total Net Direct Investment – Inward foreign direct investment minus outward foreign direct investment **NOTE – Foreign direct investment is essentially when a multinational company (MNC) invests (in physical capital) in a country other than where its operations originate. If, for example, Honda opened up a car factory in the UK, this would be considered inward foreign direct investment. If Vodafone (a UK MNC) opened up a store in the USA, this would be considered outward foreign direct investment**

Net Portfolio Investment – The value of domestic financial assets bought by foreigners minus the value of foreign financial assets bought by domestic citizens **NOTE – These could be financial assets such as shares in companies (e.g. shares in Microsoft, Apple etc...) or government or corporate bonds. In short, bonds are pieces of paper from governments or companies that allow them to borrow money off of you, based on the promise that they will return that money to you someday plus some agreed amount of interest**

Transactions in Reserve Assets – Domestic currency, commodities (e.g. gold) or other financial capital bought by foreign countries minus foreign currencies, commodities or other financial capital bought by the domestic country **NOTE – These are known as reserve assets as countries sometimes use these to maintain fixed exchange rates and finance balance of payments imbalances (these will be discussed shortly)**

Capital Account – An account identifying transactions, in the form of physical capital, between the residents of a country and the rest of the world **NOTE – It is by far the smallest account**

Balance of Payments Imbalance – A deficit or surplus on any of the accounts contained in the balance of payments e.g. a current account deficit combined with a surplus on the financial account and capital account would be an imbalance NOTE – The balance of payments is the sum of all of the accounts (current account, financial account and capital account). This sum, in theory, must be equal to 0, so if you have a large deficit on the current account of -£70bn, then the sum of the financial account and capital account must equal to £70bn. Technically speaking, the financial account could have a surplus of £74bn and the capital account a deficit of -£4bn (this would suffice), but the capital account is so small that we tend to only really care about the current account and financial account. In reality, however, mistakes do get made and there are sometimes accounting errors. This is why there is a 'net errors and omissions' section in the balance of payments, as it holds a value which will make the total sum of the balance of payments equal to 0 (to adjust for mistakes)

Protectionism – The protection of domestic industries from foreign competition e.g. this is done through trade barriers such as tariffs, quotas, subsidising exporters etc…

Tariffs – Taxes on imports

Quotas – Physical limits on the quantity of imports

International Competitiveness – The degree to which a country can, under free market conditions, meet the test of international markets, while simultaneously maintaining and expanding real income

Export-Led Growth – A strategy for achieving high and rapid economic growth through the stimulation of export activity

RIPES (Causes of Current Account Surpluses):

R – Recessions – This could lead to domestic producers struggling to sell products domestically, and so they may compete harder in international markets leading to higher export revenue. Import expenditure is also likely to fall due to the falling incomes which will decrease consumption and thus the quantity demanded of imports. This would improve (make more positive) the trade balance on the current account, which could cause a current account surplus

I – High Investment Income – The profits coming home from overseas branches of firms (branches of an MNC owned by a domestic citizen), the interest from money held in banks overseas and/or dividends from equity stakes / shares in foreign firms (not created by domestic citizens) can cause current account surpluses, if they are in high levels, as primary income will be higher as a result

P – Protectionism – Protectionism in the form of tariffs (taxes on imports), for example, would likely lead to lower import expenditure as imports would be less price competitive against domestically produced products (as the tax would make them artificially more expensive), reducing quantity demanded for them. This would improve (make more positive) the trade balance on the current account, which could cause a current account surplus

E – Low Exchange Rate – A low exchange rate would make exports cheaper and imports more expensive. This would likely lead to an increase in export revenue due to the fact that their increased price competitiveness would likely increase the quantity demanded of exports. Conversely, it would likely lead to a decrease in import expenditure due to the fact that their reduced price competitiveness would likely reduce the quantity demanded of imports. This would improve (make more positive) the trade balance on the current account, which could cause a current account surplus

S – High Savings – If a country (one like Japan) has citizens that save a lot of money, resulting in high levels of savings in banks, this will mean that banks have more money to loan out to firms looking for funds for investment. As a result, banks are likely to be more willing to lend money (and possibly at lower interest) to firms looking to invest, which will likely increase investment levels. Higher investment levels are likely to increase capital productivity which will likely make exports cheaper. Exports will now likely be more price competitive, and imports less price competitive, resulting in higher export revenue and lower import expenditure. This would improve (make more positive) the trade balance on the current account, which could cause a current account surplus

Current Account Surpluses (Problems):

- Whilst current account surpluses can be a sign of competitiveness and growth, they can also be signs of underlying problems:
    - **Over Interdependence** – Dependency on exports for growth can make a country vulnerable to global economic slowdowns / recessions
    - **Unsustainable Economic Growth** – If a country's growth is heavily export-led, and the country is not partaking in sufficient capital investment, this can lead to very high levels of inflation which, of course, will bring with it all of its costs. Additionally, if the country exports mostly finite resources, this may harm future generations and their ability to take advantage of high levels of real output in the future. The dependency on the finite resources could potentially lead to a deep economic recession once the resources have mostly depleted and been exported
    - **Retaliation** – Whilst protectionism may work for a short period of time (to reduce import expenditure), protectionism isn't going to make other countries very happy as the country (country A) that started the protectionism is essentially decreasing their export revenue. As a result, they may place tariffs and quotas on country A's exports which will cause country A's export revenue to fall, and so in the end country A's trade balance may actually get worse and they may experience lower growth
    - **Stagnated Economic Growth** – A prolonged surplus can lead to stagnated (low or negative) economic growth due to high levels of savings and low consumption, which may be overturning the high export revenue that is being earned **NOTE – This could occur if the cause of the surplus was due to high savings in banks**

Sally Eats Chicken In Columbia (Causes of Current Account Deficits):

Sally – Structural Problems – Structural problems consist of signs of low competiveness such as low productivity, low investment, high labour costs, poor infrastructure etc... If a country has structural problems in abundance, this is likely to lead to expensive, low quality exports, meaning that exports will become both less price and quality competitive compared to imports. The resulting effect would likely be higher import expenditure and lower export revenue. This would worsen (make more negative) the trade balance on the current account, which could cause a current account deficit

Eats – High Exchange Rate – A high exchange rate would make exports more expensive and imports cheaper. This would likely lead to a decrease in export revenue due to the fact that their reduced price competitiveness would likely reduce the quantity demanded of exports. Conversely, it would likely lead to an increase in import expenditure due to the fact that their increased price competitiveness would likely increase the quantity demanded of imports. This would worsen (make more negative) the trade balance on the current account, which could cause a current account deficit

Chicken – High Levels of Consumption – If a country's citizens have a very high MPI, and the country's growth is heavily consumption-led, this means that as the country grows it is likely to increase import expenditure at a fast rate. This would worsen (make more negative) the trade balance on the current account, which could cause a current account deficit

In – Low Investment Income – The profits coming home from overseas branches of firms (branches of an MNC owned by a domestic citizen), the interest from money held in banks overseas and/or dividends from equity stakes / shares in foreign firms (not created by domestic citizens) can cause current account deficits, if they are in low levels, as primary income will be lower

Columbia – A Change in Competitiveness – If new competitors (e.g. countries like India and China) emerge, this can lead to higher import expenditure in a country. This may be due to the fact that imported goods from the new competitors may be a lot cheaper, or higher quality, than the domestically produced products in said country. This would worsen (make more negative) the trade balance on the current account, which could cause a current account deficit

Current Account Deficits (Problems):

- Current account deficits aren't always a sign of economic weakness. Whether or not a deficit is a problem depends on whether or not the current account deficit is being balanced by a financial account surplus **NOTE – There is also the capital account, but it's so small that we don't really talk about it balancing out current account deficits**
- Countries like the UK and USA manage to finance huge current account deficits due to the fact that they are seen as economically sound, which attracts FDI and portfolio investment (credits in the financial account)
- In some countries, however, a current account deficit does represent weakness in the economy, specifically in cases where the current account deficit isn't being balanced by a financial account surplus, causing it to be unsustainable
- Countries doing this are essentially living beyond their means and so borrowing to finance the difference. This leads to very high levels of foreign debt which can lead to a crisis if they don't generate enough income to pay them back

Expenditure-Switching Policies – Policies that increase the price of imports and/or reduce the price of exports in order to reduce the quantity demanded of imports and raise the quantity demanded of exports, to correct a current account deficit

Expenditure-Reducing Policies – Policies that reduce the overall level of national income in order to reduce the quantity demanded of imports and thus correct a current account deficit

Expenditure-Switching Policies:

- Three methods of expenditure-switching polices are:
  - **Lowering the exchange rate**
  - **Tariffs on imports**
  - **Subsidising exporters**
- There are, however, several problems with such policies:
  - Inelastic PED for Exports and Imports – If PED for exports and imports is inelastic, then a fall in the price of exports will reduce total revenue (export revenue) and a rise in the price of imports will increase total spending (import expenditure). This would worsen the trade balance and thus worsen the current account
  - Imported Raw Material Costs – Lower exchange rates can lead to imported raw materials rising in price. If the exported goods are using said imported raw materials, then this will likely lead to their prices rising (a sign of cost-push inflation), causing exports to actually become less price competitive. This would likely reduce export revenue, which would worsen the trade balance and thus the current account deficit
  - Retaliation and Impracticality – As mentioned previously, protectionism can lead to other countries retaliating and so they may increase their levels of protectionism. This could reduce export revenue for the country that started the protectionism off, worsening their trade balance and thus their current account as well. It may also be impractical as many countries are part of the world trade organisation (WTO), and it is against the rules (if you are a member) to engage in protectionism

Expenditure-Reducing Policies:

- Three methods of expenditure-reducing polices are:
  - **Raising taxes**
  - **Reducing government spending**
  - **Raising interest rates**
- There is, however, a problem with such policies:
  - Recession – Such policies will be reducing AD, and thus national income, in the hope of reducing import expenditure. Such policies, however, may require a large sustained recession in order to correct the current account deficit. This will have many negative effects on all economic agents and so is likely not to be worth it

NOTE – If structural problems are the main cause of a current account deficit, the deficit would need to be resolved with policies known as 'supply-side' policies that would raise productivity, reduce unit labour costs, raise investment etc... Supply-side policies will be discussed in chapter 7.3

6.2 EXCHANGE RATES

Exchange Rate – The price of a currency in terms of another currency

Freely Floating Exchange Rate – An exchange rate system whereby the price of one currency expressed in terms of another is determined by the market forces of demand and supply

Foreign Exchange (FOREX) Market – A market in which people are able to buy, sell, exchange and speculate on currencies

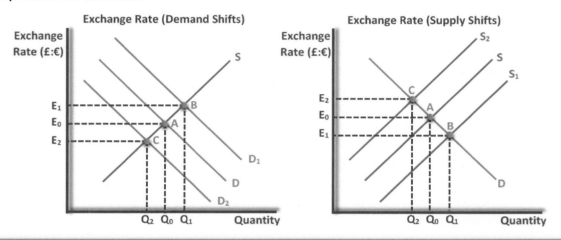

The diagrams above show how exchange rates are determined in a FOREX market. The graph on the left starts with demand being equal to supply, resulting in an exchange rate of E_0 with quantity Q_0 of the currency. An increase in demand from D to D_1, results in the exchange rate appreciating from E_0 to E_1 with quantity increasing from Q_0 to Q_1. A decrease in demand from D to D_2, results in the exchange rate depreciating from E_0 to E_2 with quantity decreasing from Q_0 to Q_2. Hence, it can be deduced that an increase in demand for a currency will have an upward pressure on the exchange rate, whilst a decrease in demand will have a downward pressure on the exchange rate (the effects on quantity aren't really important).

The graph on the right starts with demand being equal to supply, resulting in an exchange rate of E_0 with quantity Q_0 of the currency. An increase in supply from S to S_1, results in the exchange rate depreciating from E_0 to E_1 with quantity increasing from Q_0 to Q_1. A decrease in supply from S to S_2, results in the exchange rate appreciating from E_0 to E_2 with quantity decreasing from Q_0 to Q_2. Hence, it can be deduced that an increase in supply of a currency will have a downward pressure on the exchange rate, whilst a decrease in supply will have an upward pressure on the exchange rate. The suppliers of a currency are those who own the currency, and so they can increase or decrease supply depending on how much of the currency they release onto the FOREX market. The demanders of a currency are those who currently don't own the currency, and so their demand for a currency on the FOREX market can increase or decrease depending on whether or not they want more of the currency.

Appreciation – A rise in the exchange rate caused by the market forces of demand and supply in a freely floating exchange rate system

Depreciation – A fall in the exchange rate caused by the market forces of demand and supply in a freely floating exchange rate system

Hot Money – Money that is moved around the world from country to country in search of the best rate of return

SIT (Exchange Rate Determinants):

S – Speculation – If foreign currency dealers see that the UK, for example, decreases interest rates, they will expect the supply of the pound to increase, and thus the pound to depreciate, as hot money will flow out of the UK. As a result, speculators may try and sell their pounds in advance to minimise the amount of money they lose which, in the end, will cause the supply of the pound to increase further, thus causing the pound to depreciate further NOTE – Speculation can also be very sentiment driven. A recent example of this is when the pound fell sharply by about 10% after the Brexit vote, whereby traders simply began to panic, even though there was no change (at that initial point in time) in the economic performance of the UK

I – Interest Rates – If a country's interest rate rises, relative to other countries, said country will become a more attractive place in which to deposit money in banks. This will lead to hot money flowing into the country, which would mean that there has been an increase in demand for the currency (e.g. you need to have pounds to store money in a UK bank). This could then lead to the exchange rate appreciating. Conversely, if a country's interest rate falls, relative to other countries, said country will become a less attractive place in which to deposit money in banks. This will lead to hot money flowing out of the country as people search for better rates of return in other countries, which would mean that there would have been an increase in supply of said currency as people would need to sell their currency in order to buy other ones. This could then lead to the exchange rate depreciating

T – Trade – If, for any reason, there is an increase in the demand for exports, for example, this means that more people want to purchase said exports. In order to do so, they will need to sell their own currency, and then demand the new currency they want. In doing so, this increase in demand for the currency (of the country that experienced the higher demand for exports) can cause the country's exchange rate to appreciate. If, for any reason, there is an increase in demand for imports from domestic citizens, for example, this means that more domestic citizens want to purchase foreign goods (let's say that the increase in demand for imports is specifically from European countries, in this case). In order to do so, they will need to sell their own domestic currency and then buy (demand) the euro. By selling their own domestic currency they would, in essence, be increasing the supply of their domestic currency by selling it on the FOREX market, which will cause the exchange rate to depreciate NOTE – The opposite effects would of course occur if there was a decrease in demand for exports or a decrease in demand for imports. Additionally, it should be noted that, in reality, when you buy foreign goods (imports) in the UK, the store has already paid the foreign supplier and so dealt with the whole currency exchange beforehand, but the fundamental idea is the same

6.3 INTERNATIONAL TRADE

International Trade – The exchange of goods and services across international boundaries

Globalisation – The process by which the world's economies have become increasingly integrated and interdependent; the processes that have resulted in ever-closer links between the world's economies

Multinational Companies (MNCs) – Firms that control production of goods or services in one or more countries other than their home country

Foreign Direct Investment (FDI) – The establishment of branches, subsidiaries and productive processes abroad, or the purchase of foreign firms NOTE – It can also be defined as 'investment made by an MNC in a country other than where its operations originate'

World Trade Organisation (WTO) – A multilateral body that is responsible for overseeing the conduct of international trade NOTE – They have over 160 members (including the UK)

TTT (Factors Promoting Globalisation):

T – Reduced Trade Barriers – Barriers to trade, such as tariff barriers and quotas, have decreased over the years as countries have begun to realise the benefits of free trade and FDI in increasing growth rates, via increasing international trade. Organisations, such as the WTO, have also played a huge part in this by dealing with trade negotiations and ensuring that its members adhere to rules such as having no protectionist measures

T – Falling Transport Costs – Unit transport costs have been falling for the past few decades, largely due to increased innovations and privatisation of transport around the world. The bulk distribution of products, through containerisation, by sea and by air has increased hugely as a result. Economies of scale can also be taken advantage of, as vessels and aircrafts have increased in terms of both size and energy efficiency. All of this has made global sourcing increasingly viable for businesses

T – Advancements in Technology – The way in which businesses are now able to communicate via the internet has heavily increased global economic relations. This has made it easier for global supply chains to be managed (by firms) in a more effective manner. On top of that, improvements in software development have also increased the efficiency with which firms can do this

7.1 FISCAL POLICY

Fiscal Policy – The taxation and spending decisions of a government

Reflationary / Expansionary Policy – Policy measures designed to raise AD

Deflationary / Contractionary Policy – Policy measures designed to reduce AD

NOTE – Expansionary and contractionary policy can be applied to monetary policy as well

Discretionary Fiscal Policy – Deliberate changes in government spending and taxation designed to influence AD

Discretionary Fiscal Policy Measures:

- **Government Spending –** Government spending on education and training, health, or infrastructure are the main ones. Government spending on education and training can increase the human capital of those in the labour force. Improved health services mean that people shouldn't be off of work sick for so long (shorter waiting lists) and people's general health may even improve, resulting in an increase in productivity of a large number of workers. Infrastructure projects can improve transport conditions, making it cheaper and more efficient for firms to use supplier vehicles, and also for people to travel to schools, hospitals and to work in more distant places (which can further increase productivity). Such policies would increase both AD and LRAS
- **Corporation Tax –** A decrease in corporation tax, for example, would increase the amount of profits that firms can retain and use for investment, and so this would likely increase investment. Higher (net) investment increases both AD and LRAS
- **Income Tax –** A decrease in income tax, for example, would lead to an increase in disposable income for a majority of the population, which would likely lead to increased spending on goods and services and thus higher consumption (and thus higher AD). Further potential effects are that lower income tax may incentivise those who are economically inactive (outside of the labour force) to enter it, which would lead to an increase in LRAS due to a higher quantity of labour (larger labour force). Additionally, it is sometimes thought that lower income tax may incentivise people to work harder and work longer hours, due to the fact that they have the opportunity to earn more money than previously and because they are more motivated. If this leads to an increase in productivity, this could also increase LRAS due to a higher quality of labour
- **Expenditure Tax –** If the government decreases expenditure tax (e.g. VAT), for example, this will effectively reduce the costs of production for firms which, in the short run, would lead to an increase in SRAS. Additionally, investment may also increase due to the reduced tax burden on firms which should provide firms with more funds for investment. If (net) investment does increase, this would increase both AD and LRAS NOTE – Whether or not this counts as a fiscal policy measure or not may honestly depend on who is marking your paper (Edexcel can be picky sometimes). For such reasons, I would only use this point, about the government changing expenditure tax, if you desperately needed it for some reason

NOTE – As you can see, basically all of the fiscal policy measures can be considered 'double shifters' to some extent. If you don't know why changes in investment or government spending lead to changes in LRAS, go back to the chapter on factors affecting AD and LRAS (chapter 5)

Direct Tax – A tax which is levied on the income or profits of a person / firm e.g. income tax, corporation tax (called capital gains tax in the UK) etc...

Indirect Tax – A tax levied on spending on goods or services e.g. expenditure tax (VAT in the UK)

Progressive Tax – A tax that takes a larger percentage of income from high-income earners e.g. income tax (in the UK) NOTE – This works by having tax bands / brackets. This means that, for example, below £11,000 you pay no tax, between £11,000 and £43,000 you pay 20% on the income earned in that range, then between £43,000 and £150,000 you pay 40% on the income earned in that range, and so on. This is the nature of a progressive income tax

Regressive Tax – A tax that takes a larger percentage of income from low-income earners e.g. VAT NOTE – Taxes like VAT take a larger percentage of income from low-income earners because their disposable income is small, and so spending on goods and services takes up a larger percentage of their income. For those who are high-income earners, spending on goods and services take up a much smaller percentage of their income because their disposable incomes are much larger. As a result, the tax takes a larger percentage from low-income earners and lower percentage from high-income earners

Proportional / Flat Tax – A tax that takes the same percentage of income from all income earners

Output Gap – The difference between an economy's actual real GDP and potential real GDP NOTE – These can either be negative or positive

Negative Output Gap – Actual Real GDP < Potential Real GDP NOTE – This occurs when AD is either on the flat (horizontal) or curved part of the LRAS curve (i.e. when real output is below full capacity)

Positive Output Gap – Actual Real GDP > Potential Real GDP NOTE – This is typically not sustainable in the long run

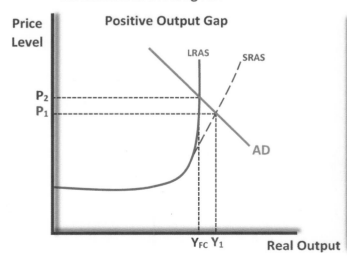

In the short run, an economy can have a positive output gap. This can be made possible by firms working workers overtime, people who are not usually in the labour force entering it temporarily, or many firms converting to the use of machinery flat out. This will likely not be sustainable in the long run, however, unless LRAS increases. It is for such reasons that most countries with positive output gaps tend to experience inflation. This is because once the short run position of real output Y_1 with price level of P_1, is over, the economy, in the long run, is constrained by full capacity level of real output Y_{FC} pushing up the price level to P_2.

Economic Cycle – The tendency for economic activity to fluctuate outside its trend growth rate, moving between high levels of economic activity (booms) and negative economic activity (recessions) NOTE – This is also known as the business cycle or the trade cycle

Trend Growth – The average rate of economic growth measured over a period of time (normally over the course of the economic cycle) NOTE – This is also known as potential growth

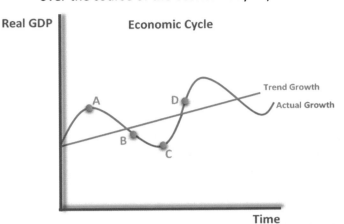

The diagram to the left shows what is known as the economic cycle. This is thought of as being a natural occurrence in an economy, but in short, basically represents what direction AD is moving in, and how fast. The point A is known as a boom (peak) and at this point, AD is actually higher than full capacity, and so there is a positive output gap. After point A, economic growth becomes negative, indicating that AD is actually falling. Point B signals the start of a slowdown (contraction), whereby the output gap has finally become negative.

Point C shows a recession (trough) occurring as now real GDP has been negative for two consecutive quarters, and so, in this case, AD will likely be falling on the horizontal part of the LRAS curve (and so the negative output gap will be at its greatest level). After point C, economic growth becomes positive again, indicating that AD is now rising and so moving towards full capacity. Point D shows a recovery (expansion) occurring, whereby the output gap has finally become positive again.

Automatic Stabilisers – Elements of fiscal policy that help to soften the impact of the economic cycle without corrective action from the government

Automatic Stabilisers:

- **Booms** – A progressive tax system means that AD can't rise as quickly in booms as it would with a flat tax system. This is due to the fact that people who are earning higher incomes are being 'slowed down' in terms of how much disposable income they can earn and then spend. This is because they will keep on entering higher and higher tax brackets that will take larger portions of their money, thus limiting rises in AD. Additionally, government spending on unemployment benefits will likely fall as the economy will likely be at full employment. This means that less money will be redistributed to the poor (who tend to have high MPCs), and so, as a result, consumption should slow down

- **Recessions** – In recessions, a progressive tax system will mean that as people earn lower incomes, they will fall into lower income tax brackets so that there spending isn't burdened as much as it would be with a flat tax system. Additionally, government spending on unemployment benefits will likely rise due to higher unemployment, and so consumption may rise as a result of more poorer people (who will likely have high MPCs) spending their money

- These effects help to reduce the fluctuation of economic activity deviating from its trend growth rate, and so the actual growth curve would be closer to the trend growth line

Government Budget – An estimation of the value of forecasted government tax revenue minus forecasted government expenditure, over a specific time period (usually a year)

Fiscal Stance / Budget Position – The government's underlying position in applying fiscal policy, and the expected impact of future taxation and government spending on the economy NOTE – This is typically measured through whether or not the budget is balanced, in surplus or in deficit

Budget Surplus – Tax Revenue > Government Expenditure

Balanced Budget – Tax Revenue = Government Expenditure

Budget Deficit – Tax Revenue < Government Expenditure

Cyclical Budget Position – The budget position in the short term. It is based on fluctuations in tax revenue and government expenditure, in accordance with the economic cycle and the operation of automatic stabilisers NOTE – This is because tax revenues will likely rise in booms (more people in higher income tax brackets) and government spending on benefits will fall in booms (due to lower unemployment), which has the tendency to lead to budget surpluses. The opposite happens in a recession, and so the tendency would be for the government to be running a budget deficit during a recession

Structural Budget Position – The budget position in the long term. It is the budget position that exists regardless of the stage of the economic cycle, due to the workings of discretionary fiscal policy NOTE – If a country is running a budget deficit of 5% (of GDP) through 'good' times and then that budget deficit worsens to 9% during a recession, it could be said that the government is running a structural budget deficit of 5%, but a cyclical deficit of 4% (9% - 5% = 4%). Similar logic could be used for a country that has a budget surplus during 'bad' times

Current Government Expenditure – Government spending on wages, raw materials and diminishable goods e.g. teacher's pay, purchase of medicine for health services etc…

Capital Government Expenditure – Government spending on capital goods and physical assets e.g. roads, bridges, hospital buildings etc…

Current Budget Position – Tax revenue minus current government expenditure

Overall Budget Position – The current budget position minus outstanding debt interest payments

National / Government Debt – The total amount of money that a central government has borrowed, and still needs to pay back; the accumulation of budget deficits, resulting in the total stock of debt (plus debt interest payments)

Government Bond – A financial asset issued by the central government as a means of borrowing money NOTE – These are also known as IOUs, which makes sense if you think about it like "I owe you [some amount] of money". IOUs are basically just pieces of paper from one economic agent (government in this case) to another (firm or consumer) saying that they will pay you periodic interest payments, and then the original amount they borrowed (e.g. £100) on the maturity date. They are typically considered the 'safest' type of loan as most governments are unlikely to default (not pay up) on their debt (depends on the country, however). There is also a principle that the prices of bonds have an inverse relationship with their interest rates (yields). This means that if a rise in demand for bonds, for example, increases their price, this will likely lead to their interest rate falling (you don't need to know the specifics for why this is the case, but do remember the principle)

Financing a Budget Deficit:

- Governments finance budget deficits by selling government bonds, which is effectively the equivalent of them borrowing money off of domestic or foreign creditors. If a government's budget position moves into a deficit, or from a deficit into a worse deficit, the government will attempt to sell more bonds so that they can borrow the required money to pay the difference between their tax revenue and expenditure

Government Borrowing (Advantages):

- **Dealing with Recessions** – During a recession, there will be lower tax revenue and higher government spending on benefits, which will contribute to a cyclical deficit automatically. If the government attempted to solve this deficit by increasing tax rates, they would likely worsen the recession and further increase unemployment. Borrowing can help an economy to finance this and get out of a recession quicker, so that they can pay it back with the tax revenues that will be earned during the cyclical budget surplus
- **Investment** – If the government borrows to increase spending on infrastructure (which is likely too costly to pay for without borrowing), for example, this can lead to an increase in the productive potential of the economy, which will enable for higher economic growth and the possibility of higher tax revenue in the future
- **Bailing Out Key Industries** – The government can borrow money to bailout banks, for example, to ensure that they don't go bankrupt and lead to a complete loss of confidence in the banking system (which could have adverse effects if it isn't stopped)

Government Borrowing (Problems):

- **Financial Crowding Out** – If the government is selling more bonds, this means that the supply of bonds is increasing. This will likely lead to the prices of said bonds falling, resulting in their interest rate rising (inverse relationship). This increased selling of bonds (by the government) can cause problems if the individuals purchasing the bonds are banks. This would be because the government would be attracting most of the potential lenders in the economy (banks) to themselves, and so these same banks may be less willing to lend to consumers and firms, or only be willing to lend to them at higher interest rates. This would then, of course, lead to lower investment and lower consumption. The resulting effects would likely be lower AD, and thus all of the problems that lower AD brings
- **Resource Crowding Out** – This type of crowding out simply means that if firms and households are buying these bonds from the government, this means that more of their 'cash' is tied up and will not come back to them for some period of time. During that period of time, firms will have less available money to invest, and consumers will have less available money to spend, causing AD to fall and, bringing with it, a host of negative effects

Correcting Budget Problems:

- **Budget Deficit** – If a government wishes to correct a budget deficit, they would likely want to do so by engaging in contractionary fiscal policy (raising taxes to get more tax revenue, and reducing government spending). This, however, may lead to lower growth, higher unemployment, and also all of the other potential negative effects of lower AD. The government will have to see if correcting the budget deficit is worth these risks

- **Budget Surplus** – If a government wishes to correct a budget surplus (unlikely, but it could happen), they would likely do so by engaging in expansionary fiscal policy (reducing taxes to get less tax revenue, and increasing government spending). This, however, could lead to high levels of inflation and also worsen the trade balance, and thus the balance of payments position potentially. The government will have to see if correcting the budget surplus is worth these risks

Fiscal Rules – Commitments by the government to limit the level of government borrowing to some amount over some period of time e.g. government borrowing can't go above 3% of GDP in a single year NOTE – The positive aspect of this, is that it may give firms and households more confidence that the government's borrowing will be sustainable. This may lead to higher consumer and business confidence, and also reduce the risk of crowding out. The downside, however, is that it may mean that in order for a government to stay committed to such rules, they will have to raise taxes during economic slowdowns or recessions which could be very damaging

Fiscal Policy Effectiveness Evaluation:

- **Depends on the Initial Level of Economic Activity** – If an economy is operating with a large amount of spare capacity, there will be virtually no effects on the price level but large effects on growth. Additionally, if the fiscal policy resulted in an increase of LRAS, and the level of AD is too low to take advantage of this, then the change in LRAS will be of little use (which could contrast with the effects of the graph you showed in your analysis in an essay). Furthermore, if the economy is operating at full capacity, the effects will be more concentrated on the price level whilst there may be no change in growth (or a somewhat small one if LRAS changes)
- **Depends on the Extent of the Discretionary Fiscal Policy** – If tax rates only go down by a small amount (or were already very low to begin with) or government spending only increases by a very small amount, for example, this will mean that the effectiveness of the fiscal policy will be limited. This would be because AD would not rise by that much, and neither would LRAS
- **Time Lag** – Discretionary fiscal policy has an overall huge time lag. Firstly, there is the recognition time lag. This occurs due to the fact that many economic indicators and reports are backwards-looking, essentially telling you what has already happened rather than what is happening now. As a result, it may take the government a very long time before they fully acknowledge the issue. Then there is the decision lag. This occurs due to the fact that government officials have to make a decision on the best course of action, which further wastes time and results in delays. Then there is the implementation lag. This is the lag time that occurs due to the time it takes for government officials to write new tax or spending laws, which, once again, wastes further time. Lastly, is the effectiveness lag. Once the policies finally feed through to the populous, it will take time for consumers and firms to fully take action in the desired manner and solve the initial problem in its entirety. All these time lags reduce the effectiveness of fiscal policy in solving economic issues, as market conditions may have changed by the time they have fed through NOTE – The time lag is even worse with government spending projects

- **Business and Consumer Confidence** – If business and consumer confidence are very low, for example, then tax cuts may not be enough to incentivise consumption and investment as people are pessimistic about future economic prospects. Additionally, in the case of higher government spending, its multiplier effect may be heavily reduced due to an increase in leakages in the form of higher savings as people, for whatever reason, don't wish to spend or invest (e.g. fears of a recession could make people weary about the dangers of accumulating debt) NOTE – The opposite could be talked about if business and consumer confidence were very high, and the government wanted to reduce AD
- **Crowding Out** – Crowding out was explained earlier in this chapter, and can be used as an evaluative point for fiscal policy if the government is increasing spending via borrowing money (selling bonds)
- **Assumes Ceteris Paribus** – This simply means that other components of AD could go in an opposing direction, or maybe the central bank could be pursuing expansionary monetary policy, whilst the government was pursuing contractionary fiscal policy. The effectiveness of fiscal policy could of course be reduced by such extra factors

7.2 MONETARY POLICY

Monetary Policy – The decisions made by the government (or central bank) in relation to monetary variables such as interest rates or the money supply

Central Bank – The entity responsible for overseeing the monetary system of a country (or group of countries) e.g. Bank of England (BoE), in the UK

Monetary Policy Committee (MPC) – A body within the Bank of England responsible for the management of monetary policy NOTE – Their inflation target is 2%

Bank Rate – The interest rate that the Bank of England pays on reserve balances held by commercial banks

Interest Rates:

- The central bank can use changes in interest rates to affect components of AD, resulting in either expansionary / inflationary or contractionary / deflationary effects. Below, are brief explanations as to how a decrease in interest rates, for example, could affect the components of AD:
    - **Consumption** – A fall in interest rates would mean that people would get less return on their savings and that it would be cheaper for people to borrow. Reduced incentive to save, combined with increased incentive to borrow, would likely increase spending on goods and services meaning that consumption would rise
    - **Investment** – There are actually four reasons as to why lower interest rates can increase investment (chapter 5.1), but the main one that is assumed is that lower interest rates mean that it will be cheaper for firms to borrow money for investment, resulting in investment increasing
    - **Net Exports (X-M)** – A decrease in interest rates will likely lead to a fall in the exchange rate (chapter 6.2). This would make exports cheaper and imports more expensive, likely leading to higher export revenue and lower import expenditure, resulting in net exports increasing

Quantitative Easing (QE) – When a central bank purchases financial assets, such as government bonds, in order to increase the money supply and lower market interest rates

Why QE May be Used:

- A central bank may undertake a policy of QE when traditional approaches to monetary policy have failed (e.g. decreasing the bank rate). This may be due to:
    - Commercial banks (e.g. Barclays, HSBC etc...) having a lot of outstanding debt and/or low cash reserves with which to lend **NOTE – Commercial banks have to keep certain levels of cash reserves in case people want to take money out of their savings accounts (e.g. they must have 10% of the value of their total loans in the form of cash reserves). Commercial banks can keep these cash reserves with the Bank of England who will then pay them an interest rate (the bank rate) on them. This means that if the bank rate is 0.5%, for example, banks have an incentive to lend more money as they will get little return from hoarding cash with the Bank of England. As a result, the commercial banks would go and loan out to firms and consumers at a slightly higher rate (e.g. 0.75% to 1%) as the commercial banks will want a higher rate than the bank rate. If, however, commercial banks are concerned about their own safety or have made all the loans they possibly can make (with their available cash reserves), the official rate may not pass on through the economy, meaning that the final market interest rate in the economy may be much higher than it should be. This would mean that even if the official bank rate had fallen to 0.5%, banks may still not give out loans, or if they did, it would be at a much higher interest rate (e.g. 5%)**
    - The second reason may simply be due to low business and consumer confidence, meaning that people simply don't want to borrow money

QE (Process):

1. The central bank creates money electronically **NOTE – You can honestly just think of this as the equivalent of some guy punching in a few keys on a computer, meaning that the central bank suddenly has 'X' amount of money to spend (e.g. 'Bank Account of Central Bank = £0' to 'Bank Account of Central Bank = £375 billion' overnight). It's just about as ridiculous as it sounds, but that is essentially all it takes for the central bank to create money. It should be noted, however, that this extra money won't do anything until it is injected into the economy**
2. This electronic money is then used to buy up financial assets (mostly government bonds) from financial institutions (mostly banks) **NOTE – The government may also buy up other assets, such as corporate bonds and other financial securities, but at this stage the central bank focuses its spending massively on government bonds, so that is where they have the largest effect**
3. The fact that the central bank is buying up lots of government bonds will mean that demand for government bonds will rise, causing their price to rise (simple demand and supply diagram effect). The relationship between bond prices and their interest rates is inverse, and so the rise in the price of government bonds will lead to lower interest rates on them
4. Two potential effects can now take place. For all of the banks that had their government bonds (pieces of paper / IOUs) replaced with cold hard cash, they may now be more

willing to lend to consumers and firms, and at lower interest rates. However, it is also possible that some of these banks may still not be willing to lend, and will still want to make large returns. They can no longer purchase government bonds because the interest rate on them has gone down, and so if they bought a government bond, the rate of return would be very low. As a result, they may decide to buy slightly riskier corporate bonds (they are riskier because a company has a higher chance, than the government, of going bankrupt and not being able to pay up), with their cold hard cash, which will have higher interest rates which said banks will like

5. This increase in the purchasing of corporate bonds will lead to an increase in their price, and thus a decrease in the interest rate for all corporate bonds (inverse relationship)

6. Once again, for all of the banks that had their corporate bonds replaced with cold hard cash, they may now be more willing to lend to consumers and firms, and at lower interest rates. The larger, more important effect, however, is that banks will now find it easier to raise finance. Banks can issue (create) their own corporate bonds as a means of borrowing money off of other individuals. As the interest rate (on corporate bonds) has fallen, this will mean that when a bank creates a new corporate bond, for themselves, the interest they will have to pay back to the lender (whoever buys the corporate bond off of them) is now lower. This means that if corporate bond interest rates fell to, for example, 0.2%, banks could now easily build up their cash reserves and then lend out to firms and consumers at a higher rate, but still a very low one (e.g. 0.5%), which would be enough for them to make a profit

7. As a result, banks on the whole (throughout this process) should now be more willing and able to lend to firms and consumers, and also at lower interest rates. The effect of the QE on the market interest rate can easily be shown on a graph

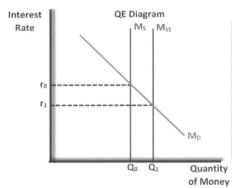

The diagram to the left shows the overall effect of QE on the market interest rate. The central bank increases the supply of money from M_S to M_{S1} (when they electronically inject money into the economy by buying the financial assets) which results in the quantity of money increasing from Q_0 to Q_1 but, more importantly, results in the market interest rate falling from r_0 to r_1.

8. The final effects are then that consumption and investment should rise (due to the lower market interest rate) which will then lead to AD increasing, and thus inflation increasing (the initial goal of all of this)

NOTE – An additional point to note, is that at stage 4 (when banks get the cold hard cash), even if they decide to go and invest the money into shares on the stock market (looking for higher returns, although there is higher risk), the effects on inflation are still likely to be positive. An increase in demand for shares will lead to the prices of shares going up, and, of course, shares are a financial asset (wealth). This can lead to a wealth effect, whereby those who owned said shares that have now seen the value of them rise will feel richer and more confident about the future of the economy, thus potentially leading to higher consumption and investment

Monetary Transmission Mechanism – The process by which monetary policy affects the inflation rate through the impact it has on other macroeconomic variables

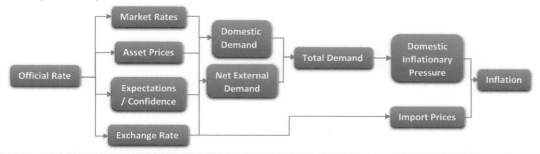

Above, is a diagram showing the basic workings of the monetary transmission mechanism. As you can see, the breakdown that was trying to be solved with QE, was the breakdown between the official rate and market rates, which led to domestic demand, specifically consumption and investment, being lower than they should have been. You can also argue that market rates also have an effect on exchange rates because if market rates don't decrease, for example, there is no reason for hot money to flow out of the country and thus no reason for the supply of the currency to increase, further meaning there is no reason for the exchange rate to depreciate. The final effect was, of course, that inflation was lower than desired, hence why the central bank may use QE to affect market rates through other means (increasing the money supply). You don't need to remember this diagram or anything like that, it's just a nice illustration of what goes on. What is worth noting, however, is that this whole process tends to take roughly about 2 years (between the official rate change and inflation), which is an important evaluative point.

Inflation Targeting – An approach to macroeconomic policy whereby the central bank is charged with meeting a target annual inflation rate that must be made known to the public

Symmetric Inflation Targeting – When deviations above and below the inflation target are given equal weight in the inflation target

Asymmetric Inflation Targeting – When deviations below the inflation target are seen to be less important than deviations above the inflation target

Inflation Targeting (Effect on the Central Bank):

- **Flexibility –** If a central bank is given a symmetric inflation target, this means that there is a degree of flexibility built into monetary policy, which can help to give the central bank time to asses and then react to a situation
- **Transparency and Accountability –** An inflation target makes the conduct of monetary policy clear, as it represents a firm commitment of price stability (by the central bank) to both firms and households. Central banks can further enhance this when they publish reasons for the decisions they make

Inflation Targeting (Effect on Firms and Households):

- **Expectations –** If the ability of the central bank to achieve the inflation target is credible, this can directly affect the expectations of inflation. If people are expecting the inflation target to be met, they may build this into their behaviour and this will do much to bring about the inflation target (i.e. expectations of inflation can become self-fulfilling) **e.g. if workers expect inflation to be high in the future, they are likely to ask for higher wage rises, increasing the likelihood of cost-push inflation**

Inflation Targeting (Problems):

- **Low Economic Growth** – The success of inflation targeting is dependent upon the central bank appearing credible, and such credibility takes time to build up. If the central bank has an asymmetric inflation target, this can lead to them trading off low economic growth for low inflation (by increasing interest rates)
- **Forecasting Difficulties** – The central bank is required to forecast where the economy will be two years from the day they enact the monetary policy. Making predictions so far into the future is likely to be highly inaccurate

Monetary Policy Effectiveness Evaluation:

- **Depends on the Initial Level of Economic Activity** – If an economy is operating with a large amount of spare capacity, there will be virtually no effects on inflation but large effects on growth. Additionally, if the monetary policy resulted in an increase of LRAS (e.g. higher investment), and the level of AD is too low to take advantage of this, the change in LRAS will be of little use (which could contrast with the effects of the graph you showed in your analysis in an essay). Furthermore, if the economy is operating at full capacity, the effects will be more concentrated on the price level whilst there may be no change in growth (or a somewhat small one if LRAS changes)
- **Depends on the Size of the Interest Rate Change** – If interest rates only go down by a small amount (or were already very low to begin with), for example, this will mean that the effectiveness of the monetary policy will be limited. This would be because AD would not rise by that much, and so inflation or growth wouldn't change by that much
- **Time Lag** – Monetary policy suffers from all the same types of lags as fiscal policy, but it suffers most greatly from the effectiveness lag. When the bank rate is initially changed, before it can affect inflation, it must go through the process known as the monetary transmission mechanism. It will first take time for commercial banks to respond to the change in policy, and thus take a very long time before this is reflected in the market interest rate. Once the interest rate has finally fed through to the populous, it will take time for consumers and firms to fully take action in the desired manner and solve whatever the initial problem was, in its entirety. This process tends to take up to about 2 years, and so this huge time lag reduces the effectiveness of monetary policy in solving economic issues. This is because market conditions are likely to have changed by the time the effects have fed through the economy NOTE – The time lag with QE is even greater
- **Low Business and Consumer Confidence** – If business and consumer confidence are extremely low, this can nullify the ability of the central bank to affect the economy via monetary policy. This would be because if consumers and firms simply don't want to borrow money but instead want to save (due to being pessimistic about future economic prospects), then they will do precisely that, even if market interest rates fall. As a result, the change in interest rates may have no effect on consumption, and thus no effect on AD, inflation or growth
- **Stock Market Bubble** – If banks react in such a way that they choose to be completely unwilling to lend, resulting in a large majority of them buying shares on the stock market (for hopes of making large returns), this could lead to an economic bubble. The increased demand for shares would result in share prices rocketing upwards, which may further attract other firms and households to put their money into the stock market. The problem with this is that these high prices would not be representative of the assets' true values

(heavily overpriced), due to the fact that people were just flocking to the market in hope of making a return, rather than due to the increasingly positive profit performance of companies. As a result, when the bubble finally does burst, due to some economic shock, prices and thus confidence will plummet, plunging said economy into a deeper recession than they would have had without this artificial boom

- **Assumes Ceteris Paribus** – This simply means that other components of AD could go in an opposing direction, or maybe that the government could be pursuing contractionary fiscal policy whilst they, the central bank, are pursuing expansionary monetary policy. The effectiveness of monetary policy could, of course, be reduced by such extra factors

Fiscal and Monetary Policy During the Great Depression and Global Financial Crisis:

- **Great Depression** – During the Great Depression (1930s), the US government (and many others) followed the classical school of economic thought, and so were determined to balance the government budget by cutting government spending. They also believed that the only way unemployment would fall would be if labour costs were reduced (so that employers would have more incentive to hire workers), and so many governments encouraged people to take wage cuts. This had the effect of heavily reducing AD and thus both economic growth and employment. It was at this time that Keynes suggested that governments ought to increase their spending and so heal the economy through the multiplier effects that would follow which, in the case of the Great Depression, worked very well

- **Global Financial Crisis (GFC)** – During the GFC of 2007/08 access to credit (e.g. loans) was very poor. Reducing the bank rate seemed to do very little to affect market interest rates and increase access to credit. It was at this time that the UK central bank, and many others around the world, began to partake in what is now called QE. QE is thought to have helped many economies recover from the GFC, but many argue that QE can potentially be very harmful and so may do more bad than good in the long run

7.3 SUPPLY-SIDE POLICIES

Demand-Side Policies – Polices designed to impact AD through changes in government spending, taxes, interest rates or the quantity of the money supply NOTE – Fiscal and monetary policy are both considered to be demand-side policies

Supply-Side Policies – Polices designed to boost LRAS by increasing the quantity and/or quality of the factors of production, or by improving the efficiency of labour and product markets

NOTE – Whether or not something is a supply-side policy depends on if it increases LRAS, and the initial intent of the policy. If the government increased spending on education and training with the raw intention of just increasing AD during a recession, you wouldn't really go saying that it was a supply-side policy. If, however, their raw intention was to increase the quality of labour and thus LRAS, then the government could be considered to be doing a supply-side policy. As a general rule of thumb, if the question wants you to talk about fiscal or monetary policy, don't mention the word supply-side policy (you can still talk about LRAS increasing, of course though), and if it wants you to talk about supply-side policies, don't mention the words fiscal or monetary policy (the examiner may think you are confused). There is overlap between them in the sense that fiscal or monetary policy can fall underneath supply-side policy, but just stick to what the question is asking about

NOTE – Supply-side polices can manifest in one of two forms: market-based policies or interventionist policies

Market-Based Policies – Policies that aim to allow markets to work more freely, and provide incentives for entrepreneurship and initiative

Interventionist Policies – Policies that tend to involve the government resolving what it believes to be market failures through increases in regulation and government spending

Supply-Side Policies:

- **Government Spending on Education and Training –** Increased government spending on education and training would increase the level of human capital and thus labour productivity. This would be a sign of an improvement in the quality of labour and also the fact that more goods and services could be produced in the same time period. This would increase the productive potential of the economy and so also cause LRAS to increase
- **Reduced Income Tax and Reduced Unemployment Benefits –** A decrease in income tax and a reduction in unemployment benefits, may incentivise those who are economically inactive (outside of the labour force) to enter it. This would be because there is now the potential to earn higher levels of disposable income and also (for the voluntary unemployed) reduced incentive to stay unemployed as their disposable income will shrink (due to lower benefits). This could lead to an increase in LRAS due to a higher quantity of labour (larger labour force) and thus increased productive potential. Additionally, it is sometimes thought that lower income tax may incentivise people to work harder and work longer hours, due to the fact that they have the opportunity to earn more money than previously and because workers may feel more motivated. If this leads to an increase in productivity, this could also increase LRAS due to a higher quality of labour
- **Reducing Marginal Tax Rates –** Similar to a decrease in income tax, this would involve the government reducing the progressive nature of the tax system, by either removing higher tax bands or reducing the tax rates in them. This could have the effect of incentivising higher levels of entrepreneurship, as people now know that the potential to earn larger levels of disposable income as an entrepreneur is higher. This increase in the quantity of entrepreneurship could increase the productive potential of the economy because entrepreneurs are likely to be able to organise and use existing resources in a more efficient manner, allowing more output to be produced from the same amount of resources. This could then, of course, lead to LRAS increasing
- **Introducing a NMW or increasing a NMW to a NLW (National Living Wage) –** An introduction of a NMW, may incentivise those who are economically inactive (outside of the labour force) to enter it because there would now be the potential to earn higher levels of disposable income. This could lead to an increase in LRAS due to a higher quantity of labour (larger labour force) and thus increased productive potential NOTE – Another point to bear in mind is that if you were to draw the potential positive effects on a AD/LRAS graph, you may want to show AD increasing (as well as LRAS). This is due to the fact that a NMW or NLW may now suggest that people will have higher disposable incomes, leading to higher consumption and thus AD. For evaluation, you could say that a policy like this would likely just lead to classical unemployment, and

that the increase in labour supply would simply make it worse. You could also argue that it could lead to a fall in (net) investment due to firms' retained profits falling (due to higher costs) which could decrease both AD and LRAS

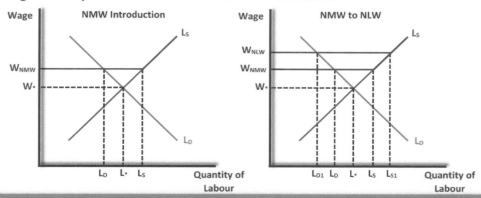

The diagram on the left shows that the introduction of the NMW results in classical unemployment of $L_S - L_D$, compared to the free market outcome that produced employment of L* (a better employment situation). This would be happening across a range of labour markets and so whilst you may see an increase in LRAS (productive potential), an increased amount of unemployed people is likely to lead to lower consumption and thus, potentially, lower AD. The diagram on the right shows similar effects with classical unemployment increasing from $L_S - L_D$ to $L_{S1} - L_{D1}$ (once the NLW is imposed) which, compared to the free market outcome, is considerably worse. The potential of AD falling here would also occur. In both cases, an increase in labour supply (caused by an increase in the size of the labour force) would actually make the classical unemployment even worse (it's not on the diagrams because they would get somewhat cramped / confusing if labour supply was increasing on them). Bear in mind that these are evaluative points for an essay in which you were initially arguing that a NMW, or NLW, is a positive supply-side policy.

- **Removing a NMW** – You could also make the case that removing a NMW could be considered a supply-side policy. Removing a NMW would reduce the costs of production of many firms, likely resulting in an increase in their profit margins and thus retained profits. Firms may then feel more willing and able to increase investment, and the higher profit margins may increase business confidence, further increasing firms' willingness to invest. This could result in both AD and LRAS increasing (LRAS would increase due to a larger capital stock). Additionally, you could also say that the fall in classical unemployment (because the NMW is gone) would mean that rather than people receiving benefits, some people would now be receiving wages and thus likely higher disposable incomes (than the benefits they were on) after the NMW is removed. This could lead to an increase in consumption and thus AD **NOTE – As you can see NMWs (or NLWs) are tricky in the sense that you can argue a lot of things, based on what you think the domineering effects are**

- **Improving Labour Market Flexibility** – A flexible labour market is one that adjusts quickly and smoothly to changes in the demand and supply of labour. Labour markets that are not flexible are often characterised with high geographical and occupational immobility, which lead to structural unemployment. The government could reduce geographical immobility by increasing information provision of available jobs in different regions, giving people (whose skills are needed in other regions) grants or loans to move to other areas, subsidising rented accommodation provided by councils (in an attempt to reduce housing costs), increasing spending on transport infrastructure (so that it is easier to move between regions), or by subsidising firms to move to areas with high regional unemployment. The government could reduce occupational immobility mostly by increasing spending on education and training, which would provide more people with the necessary skills and qualifications to get jobs that they are currently locked out of. Reducing geographical immobility would increase the quantity of labour (due to a larger labour force) and reducing occupational immobility would potentially increase both the quantity and quality of labour, due to more people entering the labour force and an increase in the levels of human capital. This would mean that the ability of the economy to produce goods and services would increase, causing the productive potential of the economy to increase and thus LRAS

- **Relaxing Immigration Laws** – Relaxing immigration laws would likely lead to an increase in the amount of immigration a country experiences. An increase in the number of immigrants (assuming most of them are of working age) would lead to an increase in the size of the labour force. This would increase the quantity of labour and thus the productive potential of the economy, and so LRAS as well. It would also lead to an increase in AD as there would be more people earning disposable incomes and thus higher consumption

- **Increased Privatisation** – Privatisation is the transfer of ownership of property or business (e.g. the NHS) from a government to the private sector. It is often thought that the government can be inefficient in its use of resources and so, as a result, productive potential will be lower than it should be due to wasteful use of resources. By transferring some of these resources to the private sector, it is thought that the productive potential of the economy may increase. This is because firms will likely use said resources more efficiently due to their profit incentive and their incentive to not be wasteful and let costs get out of control. They may also provide better quality products due to the fact that they will be specialised in the product that they are producing (unlike government officials), and so this can further increase the productive potential of the economy and thus LRAS

- **Deregulation** – Deregulation is likely to reduce the costs of production for firms (which should increase their profit margins), and it may also make them more optimistic about future economic conditions as they can potentially look forward to more deregulatory policies from the government rather than being fearful of more regulatory ones. The resulting effect would potentially be an increase in (net) investment which would increase both AD and LRAS. An additional effect, is that decreased regulations should reduce barriers to entry which may have been preventing new technology or more efficient producers from entering the market. As a result, this could have the effect of incentivising higher levels of entrepreneurship and improved technology, which could increase the productive potential of the economy and thus lead to LRAS increasing

- **Trade Union Reform** – Increasing legislation towards trade unions (giving them more power) would effectively have the same potential positive and negative effects of a NMW (in the case of drawing the labour market diagram, you would just write W_{TU} instead of W_{NMW}, as trade unions can end up pushing wages above equilibrium). Reducing legislation towards trade unions / increasing legislation against them (reducing their power) would have virtually the same effects as a reduction in NMW (or an abolition of the NMW) NOTE – A trade union is a labour organisation that seeks to promote the interest of its members (they often deal with wage negotiations with employers)

- **Government Spending on Infrastructure** – Increased government spending on infrastructure is largely to do with the improvement of access to energy and improvement of transport links (e.g. roads, trains etc...). In the case of improvements in energy infrastructure, this is likely to reduce costs for firms in obtaining energy and may also result in a rise in efficiency. In the case of improvements in transport, this may improve transport conditions, making it cheaper and more efficient for firms to use supplier vehicles, and also for people to travel to schools, hospitals and to work in more distant places (which can further increase productivity). The increased efficiency of firms (higher productivity) will increase productive potential, and the increased ease of travelling for individuals is likely to lead to improvements in both the quality of labour (due to higher labour productivity) and possibly the quantity of labour (due to the geographically immobile people now entering the labour force), which would both also increase productive potential and thus LRAS

- **Research and Development (R&D) Incentives and Subsidies** – If the government encourages, supports and funds more science education in schools and science research in universities, this can lead to improvements in technology (the quality of capital) which would increase productive potential and thus LRAS. The government could also subsidise firms, as that would effectively reduce their costs of production, which would increase their profit margins and thus their retained profits. These retained profits could either be used for increased investment in capital goods and/or increased investment in R&D. This would increase both the quantity and quality of capital, increasing productive potential and thus LRAS

Supply-Side Policies Effectiveness Evaluation:

- **Depends on the Initial Level of Economic Activity** – If an economy is operating with a large amount of spare capacity, then an increase of LRAS will be of little use if the level of AD is too low to take advantage of it (which could contrast with the effects of the graph you showed in your analysis in an essay). The usefulness of a supply-side policy will be greatest when the initial level of economic activity is very high

- **Depends on the Size of the Change** – If, for example, the size of a subsidy that the government gave to firms (in some industry) was very small, this will limit the impact it has on their costs of production, their profits, their level of investment (in capital or R&D), and thus the impact on LRAS. This would reduce the effectiveness of such a policy

- **Opportunity Cost** – Supply-side policies that involve subsidies or government spending are extremely expensive, often costing billions of pounds. This is money that could have been spent on other essential services such as health services or education. Possibly, the government actually funded this through cuts in spending on health or education, and so they would be creating new problems in those areas. Additionally, if the government spending or subsidy was paid for through borrowing, then the government will have to pay this back in the future by raising taxes (to increase tax revenue). Higher taxes (particularly corporation tax) could then end up reducing productive potential, and thus LRAS, due to its negative impact on investment NOTE – If the government, in your specific essay answer, spent money on education, then the opportunity cost of it would be the potential lost spending on healthcare (or transport) or the cuts made in them. You would just flip the examples around depending on what your specific question was

- **Time Lag** – Supply-side policies suffer from all the same types of lags as fiscal policy and monetary policy, although it suffers most greatly from the implementation and effectiveness lag. Supply-side policies that involve government spending require a very long time to even set up. For example, it may take up to a decade to build lots of new schools, and spending on infrastructure could potentially take multiple decades. Even in the case (for spending on education) when it mostly consists of reforms to the education system, before the full effects of those reforms can be felt and then seen to increase the level of human capital, it could take decades (or even longer, depending on what level of education is getting reformed). Such large time lags reduce the effectiveness of supply-side policies **NOTE – In the case that the supply-side policy involves taxes or interest rates, it would then have exactly the same time lags as fiscal or monetary policy. This means that in order to stretch out your answer, you could talk more specifically about the time lags involved in, for example, reducing interest rates (if the supply-side policy was based on interest rates)**

- **No Guarantee of Success** – Almost all of these supply-side policies could largely be said to be based upon fairly wishful thinking. In reality, there is no guarantee that people will react or behave in the way that the government expects them to (e.g. low or high business and/or consumer confidence). The government's policy itself may even be flawed (e.g. wasteful education reforms that do little to improve the quality of education)

- **Assumes Ceteris Paribus** – This simply means that opposing factors, that were initially ignored, may actually reduce the effectiveness of a supply-side policy. For example, maybe a supply-side policy based on reducing corporation tax (to increase investment and thus the size of the capital stock), is being run while the central bank is pursuing contractionary monetary policy (e.g. increasing interest rates) which actually reduce the incentive to invest. The domineering effect will decide whether or not the supply-side policy is successful or not, but the bottom line is that its effectiveness could very well be limited by other factors that have nothing to do with the policy

7.4 POLICY CONFLICTS

Policy Conflict – Occurs when two economic policy objectives cannot both be achieved at the same time, or at least not through the modification of AD alone in the short run; the better the performance in achieving one policy objective, the more difficult it is to achieve high performance in the other

Policy Conflicts (Trade-Offs):

- **Low Unemployment and Low Inflation** – In trying to lower unemployment but also keep inflation at a low and stable rate, you would struggle to do so via increasing AD alone **SOLUTION – Increase both AD and LRAS so that you can get both a rise in real output (and thus employment) and potentially only a small rise or even no change in inflation (depending on how much LRAS shifts out)**

- **High Growth and Low Inflation** – In trying to achieve high growth but also keep inflation at a low and stable rate, you would struggle to do so via increasing AD alone **SOLUTION – Increase both AD and LRAS so that you can get both a rise in real output (and thus short run economic growth) and potentially only a small rise or even no change in inflation (depending on how much LRAS shifts out)**

- **Higher Inflation and a Satisfactory Balance of Payments Position** – In trying to increase inflation (because it is currently lower than desired) but also trying to achieve a satisfactory balance of payments position, this would likely be very difficult through increasing AD alone. This is because firstly, higher inflation would make exports less price competitive and make imports more price competitive (compared to domestically produced products), likely resulting in lower export revenue, higher import expenditure, a worsened trade balance and thus a worsened current account position. Secondly, would be due to the fact that if the higher inflation is caused by rises in consumption (that increased AD), and the country's citizens have a high MPC, they may begin increasing their import expenditure, which may not be enough to counter the consumption on domestic goods (so AD will still rise and so will inflation), but the trade balance would be worsening as a result SOLUTION – Increase both AD and LRAS so that even if inflation rises, better technology may increase the quality of exports, or higher productivity may mean that the average costs to producers who make exports will fall. As a result, the country could still become internationally competitive despite having slightly higher inflation (the effect on inflation depends on the size of the shift in LRAS) NOTE – Another potential view on this would be that if you wanted low inflation, such a goal may be difficult to pursue if you are trying to improve your balance of payments position by increasing export revenue, as that would increase AD and thus inflation

- **Higher Growth and a Satisfactory Balance of Payments Position** – In trying to increase growth but also trying to achieve a satisfactory balance of payments position, this would likely be very difficult through increasing AD alone. This is because firstly, higher growth would likely lead to higher inflation which would make exports less price competitive and make imports more price competitive (compared to domestically produced products), likely resulting in lower export revenue, higher import expenditure, a worsened trade balance and thus a worsened current account position. Secondly, would be due to the fact that if the higher growth is caused by rises in consumption, and the country's citizens have a high MPC, they may begin increasing their import expenditure, which may not be enough to counter the consumption on domestic goods (so AD would still rise and so would growth), but the trade balance would be worsening as a result SOLUTION – Increase both AD and LRAS so that real output can increase and inflation can fall (if LRAS shifts out far enough to the right). Additionally, if the rise in LRAS is caused by better technology or higher productivity then exports may become more price or quality competitive, and so the country could become more internationally competitive (leading to a better trade balance and thus a better current account)

Phillips Curve – An economic concept that shows that inflation and unemployment have an empirical inverse relationship, further suggesting that there is a trade-off between the two in any economy

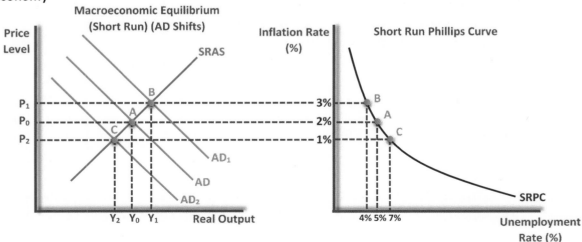

The short run Phillips curve (SRPC) is a representation of a trade-off that is well known to many of us today. This is the trade-off between unemployment and inflation. The Phillips curve suggests that at low rates of unemployment, labour is scarcer and so employers are more willing to bid up their wage rates in order to get said labour, resulting in higher inflation as higher wages are thought to get passed onto consumers in the form of higher prices. The opposite is thought to happen with high unemployment rates, and so this results in a downwards sloping SRPC on the right diagram. As we have discussed previously in this book, higher levels of AD tend to increase employment (i.e. decrease unemployment), but with the cost of higher inflation. How AD effects unemployment and inflation can be represented well through the use of the diagrams on the previous page. The left diagram starts with AD being equal to SRAS, resulting in a price level of P_0 at real output level of Y_0, further resulting in an inflation rate of 2% combined with an unemployment rate of 5%. An increase in AD from AD to AD_1 results in real output increasing from Y_0 to Y_1 and the price level rising from P_0 to P_1, causing the inflation rate to rise from 2% to 3% and unemployment to fall from 5% to 4%. On the contrary, a fall in AD from AD to AD_2 results in real output falling from Y_0 to Y_2 and the price level falling from P_0 to P_2, causing the inflation rate to fall from 2% to 1% and unemployment to rise from 5% to 7%. The takeaway from this is to realise that whenever AD shifts right or left there is a movement along the SRPC, and so the SRPC can effectively be used as a potential way of showing how demand-pull inflation takes place (higher AD → higher demand for labour as it is a derived demand → **higher employment** but also higher wages → **higher inflation**).

Stagflation – When an economy experiences both high unemployment and high inflation at the same time

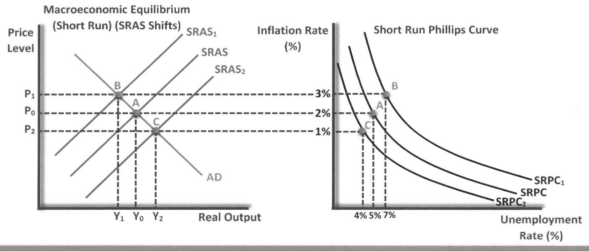

Stagflation occurs when AS (SRAS in this case) shifts to the left, as it creates both higher inflation and lower employment (i.e. higher unemployment). The effects of shifts in SRAS on the SRPC can be shown using the diagrams above. The left diagram starts with AD equal to SRAS resulting in a price level of P_0 with real output of Y_0, combined with an inflation rate of 2% and an unemployment rate of 5%. A shift in SRAS from SRAS to $SRAS_1$ results in the price level rising from P_0 to P_1 with real output decreasing from Y_0 to Y_1, causing inflation to rise from 2% to 3% and unemployment to rise from 5 to 7%. SRPC shifts from SRPC to $SRPC_1$ to represent this, as the initial SRPC would have claimed that the fall in SRAS would result in lower unemployment (which isn't the case), and so SRPC has shifted right to represent the fact that there is both higher inflation and higher unemployment. On the contrary, an increase in SRAS from SRAS to $SRAS_2$ results in the price level falling from P_0 to P_2 with real output increasing from Y_0 to Y_2, causing inflation to decrease from 2% to 1% and unemployment to decrease from 5% to 4%. SRPC simply shifts left from SRPC to $SRPC_2$ to represent this. Hence, it can be deduced that shifts in SRAS cause shifts in the SRPC, which, more specifically, allow changes in cost-push inflation to be shown on a SRPC diagram.

NOTE – There are many potential policy conflicts that can occur. If you are ever asked about any of them, chances are that an increase in both AD and LRAS is needed in order to satisfy both objectives. Bear in mind, however, that policy conflicts between monetary and fiscal policy are more troublesome and could be more difficult to solve, depending on what both of the policies are trying to achieve

1.1 THE FUNDAMENTALS OF ECONOMICS

Economics – The study of how to most effectively allocate scarce resources

Microeconomics – The study of individual economic agents and their decision making

Scarcity – A situation where there are insufficient resources to meet people's unlimited wants

Sustainability – Using resources so as not to compromise future generations' standard or quality of life

Goods – Tangible products that can be touched and measured e.g. cars, food, washing machines

Services – Intangible products that cannot be touched or measured e.g. banking, insurance, healthcare

Utility – The total satisfaction received from consuming a good or service

Needs – Goods or services that are required to maintain existence / life e.g. food, water, shelter

Wants – Goods or services that we desire but are not necessary for maintaining existence / life e.g. cars, watches, TVs

Renewable Resources – Natural resources of economic value that can be replaced or replenished, or simply aren't used up e.g. wood, solar energy, wind energy

Non-Renewable Resources – Natural resources of economic value that cannot be readily replaced by natural means on a level equivalent to their consumption e.g. oil, natural gas, coal

Positive Statements – Statements that do not have to be correct, but must be able to be tested, and proved or disproved e.g. the UK's annual GDP growth rate was 2% in January 2016

Normative Statements – Statements that are opinion based and so cannot be proved or disproved e.g. the government should provide basic education to all citizens

1.2 OPPORTUNITY COST AND ECONOMIC AGENTS

Opportunity Cost – The potential value of the next-best alternative, which is forgone when a choice is made

Economic Goods – Goods that impose some cost on society when produced. They are scarce / limited, and so have opportunity cost e.g. TVs, cars, chairs etc...

Free Goods – Goods that impose no cost on society when produced. They are unlimited, and so have no opportunity cost e.g. air, sunlight etc...

Economic Agents – Decision makers that have effects on the economy of a country by buying, producing, selling, investing, taxing etc... e.g. households, firms and governments

Household – A group of consumers that buy goods and services. They also supply their labour to firms to produce goods and services, in order to earn the income needed to purchase goods and services

Firm – An organisation that uses factors of production alongside each other in order to produce output. They produce goods and services demanded by consumers

Government – A governing body / organisation that undertakes expenditure (spending) and impacts the economy via taxation and the regulation of markets

1.3 FACTORS OF PRODUCTION AND PRODUCTION POSSIBILITY CURVES (PPCS)

Factors of Production – The available resource inputs used in the production process of goods and services

Factors of Production (CELL) – Capital + Entrepreneurship + Labour + Land

Capital – Man-made aids for production; goods used to make other goods e.g. MERC – Machines + Equipment + Robots + Computers

Entrepreneurship – The willingness of an entrepreneur to take risks and organise production

Labour – The human resource that is available in an economy; the quantity and quality of human resources

Land – The natural resource that is available in an economy; the quantity and quality of natural resources e.g. oil, coal, rivers, the land itself etc…

Consumer Goods – Goods bought and used by consumers for present use; final goods used for consumption means rather than production ones e.g. food, TVs, cars, watches etc…

Model – A simplified representation of reality used to create hypotheses (or theories) about economic decisions and events

Production Possibility Curve (PPC) – A curve showing the maximum quantities of different combinations of goods and/or services that can be produced in a set time period, given available resources and the current state of technology

1.4 SPECIALISATION AND THE FUNCTIONS OF MONEY

Specialisation – The focusing by a worker or workers, firm, region or whole economy on the production of a narrow range of products

Division of Labour – A process whereby the production process is broken down into a series of stages, and workers are designated to particular stages

Productivity – Output of a good or service, per factor of production, per period of time

Money – The circulating medium of exchange as defined by a government

Barter System – A system that relies on the exchange of goods and services for other goods and services, without the use of money e.g. a potato farmer trading a sack of potatoes for a cut of beef

2.1 RESOURCE ALLOCATION AND THE OBJECTIVES OF ECONOMIC AGENTS

Resource Allocation – The way in which a society's factors of production are used amongst their alternative uses

Utility Maximisation – The aim of trying to achieve the highest level of satisfaction possible

Profit Maximisation – The aim of trying to achieve the highest level of profit possible

Market Economy – An economy in which the market forces of demand and supply determine the allocation of resources

Centrally Planned Economy – An economy in which the state determines the allocation of resources

Mixed Economy – An economy in which both the market forces of demand and supply, and also the operation of the state, determine the allocation of resources

Capitalism – An economic system characterised by the private ownership of productive resources, and the ability of individuals to freely pursue their self-interest with minimal interference from the government

2.2 THE NATURE AND CHARACTERISTICS OF DEMAND

Demand – The quantity of a good or service that consumers are willing and able to purchase at any possible price in a given time period

Ceteris Paribus – A Latin phrase that means 'other things being equal'

Law of Demand – A law that states that, ceteris paribus, there is an inverse relationship between the quantity demanded and price of a good or service

Notional Demand – The desire or want for a product

Effective Demand – The willingness and ability to buy a product

Demand Curve – A graph that shows how much of a product will be demanded at any given price

Demand Schedule – The collection of data that is used to draw a demand curve for a product

Market – A place in which there are a set of arrangements allowing transactions to take place between buyers and sellers

Sub-Market – A recognised or distinguishable geographic, economic or specialised subdivision of a market, also known as a market segment

Composite Demand – Demand for a good that has various uses e.g. water (drinking, washing etc...)

Diminishing Marginal Utility – A situation whereby an individual gains less additional utility from consuming a product, the more of it they consume

Veblen / Snob Good – A good for which the quantity demanded increases as the price increases, because of its exclusive nature and allure as a status symbol e.g. designer, luxury items with a strong brand identity such as a Rolex watch

Elasticity – A measure of a variable's sensitivity relative to a change in another variable

Price Elasticity of Demand (PED) – A measure of the responsiveness of quantity demanded relative to a change in the price of a good or service

Price Elasticity of Demand (PED) Formula(s) – $\frac{\% \text{ change in quantity demanded}}{\% \text{ change in price}}$ OR $\frac{\text{Original Price}}{\text{Original Quantity Demanded}} \times \frac{\text{numerical change in quantity demanded}}{\text{numerical change in price}}$

Price Inelastic Demand – Where the percentage change in the quantity demanded of a product is insensitive to a change in the price of the product ($0 <|PED|< 1$) e.g. if the price of Starbucks coffee increased, there would be a fall in the amount of units (of coffee) they sold, but it would likely be a very small one due to the brand loyalty and addiction many of us have to companies like Starbucks and their products

Price Elastic Demand – Where the percentage change in the quantity demanded of a product is sensitive to a change in the price of the product ($|PED| > 1$) e.g. if the price of Walkers crisps increased, you may feel inclined to buy a lot less as there are a lot of other substitutes in the form of other crisp packet brands and also in the form of other snacks (e.g. peanuts, biscuits)

Price Unitary Elastic Demand – Where the percentage change in the quantity demanded of a product is equal to a change in the price of the product ($|PED|= 1$)

Percentage Change Formula – $\frac{\text{New Figure}-\text{Old Figure}}{\text{Old Figure}} \times 100$

Total Revenue (TR) – The total amount of money received for goods sold or services provided over a certain time period

Total Revenue (TR) Formula – $Price \times Quantity$

Income Elasticity of Demand (YED) – A measure of the responsiveness of quantity demanded relative to a change in income

Income Elasticity of Demand (YED) Formula – $\frac{\% \text{ change in quantity demanded}}{\% \text{ change in income}}$

Income Inelastic Demand – Goods for which a change in income produces a less than proportionate change in quantity demanded ($|YED|< 1$)

Income Elastic Demand – Goods for which a change in income produces a greater than proportionate change in quantity demanded ($|YED| > 1$)

Income Unitary Elastic Demand – Goods for which a change in income produces a proportionate change in quantity demanded ($|YED| = 1$)

Normal Good – A good where the quantity demanded increases when income rises (YED > 0)

Superior (Luxury) Good – A good where the quantity demanded increases by a proportionately greater amount than a rise in income (YED > 1) e.g. iPhones (you are likely to buy a lot more if your income rises)

Necessity Good – A good where the quantity demanded increases by a proportionately smaller amount than a rise in income (0 < YED < 1) e.g. bread (if your income rose you probably wouldn't spend that much more money on bread)

Inferior Good – A good where the quantity demanded decreases when income rises (YED < 0) e.g. bus travel (if your income rises, you are more likely to spend less on bus travel and just travel by taxi or a personal car instead)

Giffen Good – A good where the quantity demanded decreases by a proportionately greater amount than a rise in income (YED < -1) e.g. YED = -2: income rises by 10% → quantity demanded for good (Giffen good) falling by 20%

Substitutes – Products that can be used for a similar purpose, such that if the price of one product rises, demand for the other product is likely to rise e.g. PS4 and Xbox One

Complements – Products that tend to be consumed jointly, such that if the price of one product rises, demand for the other product is likely to fall e.g. PS4 and PS4 video games, or tea and milk

Competitive Demand – Demand for products that are competing with each other

Joint Demand – Demand for products which are interdependent, such that they are jointly demanded

Cross Elasticity of Demand (XED) – A measure of the responsiveness of quantity demanded for one product relative to a change in the price of another product

Cross Elasticity of Demand (XED) Formula – $\dfrac{\% \ change \ in \ quantity \ demanded \ of \ product \ X}{\% \ change \ in \ price \ of \ product \ Y}$

Substitutes (XED Terminology) – Products which have a positive XED value

Complements (XED Terminology) – Products which have a negative XED value

Marginal Social Benefit (MSB) – The additional benefit that society gains from consuming one more unit of a product

Consumer Surplus – The extra amount of money that a consumer is willing to pay for a product above the price that they actually pay

2.3 THE NATURE AND CHARACTERISTICS OF SUPPLY

Supply – The quantity of a good or service that producers are willing and able to offer at different market prices over a period of time

Law of Supply – A law that states, ceteris paribus, there is a direct relationship between the quantity supplied and price of a good or service

Supply Curve – A graph showing how much of a product will be supplied at any given price

Supply Schedule – The collection of data used to draw the supply curve of a product

Competitive Market – A market in which individual firms cannot influence the market price of the product they are selling, because of the high competition from other firms

Competitive Supply – When a firm can use its factors of production to produce more than one type of product e.g. a firm can use land to supply food or instead divert its use of land to producing bio-fuels

Composite Supply (Rival Supply) – When supply of a product comes from more than one source; a product whose demand can be satisfied through various sources e.g. electricity is a composite supply as it can be made from gas, nuclear power, wind turbines, hydroelectric turbines etc... All these sources contribute to make up the supply of electricity, and thus the demand for electricity can be satisfied through the supply of gas, nuclear power etc... There is competition between them and so the most economical source is used first (and used the most), but in the end the rest are combined to co-operate and contribute to the supply of said product

Joint Supply – When a firm can produce more than one type of product with roughly the same factors of production e.g. the supply of beef and leather are linked because both of them are made using cows

Price Elasticity of Supply (PES) – A measure of the responsiveness of quantity supplied relative to a change in the price of a good or service

Price Elasticity of Supply (PES) Formula – $\dfrac{\% \ change \ in \ quantity \ supplied}{\% \ change \ in \ price}$

Price Inelastic Supply – Where the percentage change in the quantity supplied of a product is insensitive to a change in the price of the product (0 < PES < 1) e.g. if the price of a commodity, such as oil, increases, an oil company will be slow to increase supply as it takes a long time to drill oil out from the ground

Price Elastic Supply – Where the percentage change in the quantity supplied of a product is sensitive to a change in the price of the product (PES > 1) e.g. if a car factory is operating at 60% of full capacity, then the car company could easily increase the quantity supplied of cars if there was an increase in price, and so would likely do so, very quickly, and to a great extent, relative to the size of the increase in price

Price Unitary Elastic Supply – Where the percentage change in the quantity supplied of a product is equal to a change in the price of the product (PES = 1)

Marginal Cost (MC) – The cost of producing one more unit of output

Producer Surplus – The difference between the price that a firm is willing to accept for a product and the price that they actually receive for the product

2.4 MARKET EQUILIBRIUM AND THE PRICE MECHANISM

Free Market Mechanism – The mechanism by which the market forces of demand and supply determine prices and the economic decisions made by consumers and firms

Price – The sum of money that is paid for a given quantity of a particular product

Price System / Mechanism – The method of allocating resources via the free movement of prices

Market Equilibrium / Clearing Price – A situation that occurs in a market when the price is such that the quantity that consumers are willing to buy is equal to the quantity that firms are willing to supply

Disequilibrium – When internal or external forces prevent market equilibrium from being reached, such that the market is in a position where demand and supply are not equal

Surplus – An excess of supply (quantity supplied) over demand (quantity demanded)

Shortage – An excess of demand (quantity demanded) over supply (quantity supplied)

Derived Demand – Demand for a factor of production or good which derives not from the factor or good itself, but from the product(s) it can produce; demand for one item depending on demand for another e.g. labour is not wanted for its own sake, but for the level of output it can produce and what that output can be sold for

Unemployment – Occurs when someone of working age is out of work and actively seeking work

Exchange Rate – The price of one currency in terms of another currency

Interest Rate – The cost of borrowing money, and the amount paid for lending money (or saving)

Comparative Static Analysis – Examines the effect on equilibrium of a change in the external factors affecting a market

2.5 EFFICIENCY

Production – A process, or sequence of processes, that convert factor inputs into output

Short Run – The time period when at least one factor of production, usually capital, is fixed in quantity e.g. a firm does not have time to sell off its existing building, end a renting contract, extend an existing building or acquire a new building in the short run

Long Run – The time period when the quantities of all factors of production are variable

Productive Efficiency – Attained when a firm produces at minimum average total cost (ATC), choosing a suitable combination of inputs (cost efficiency) and producing the maximum possible output from those inputs (technical efficiency); where production takes place using the least amount of scarce resources

Cost Efficiency – The suitable combination of inputs of factors of production, given the relative prices of said factors

Technical Efficiency – Producing the maximum possible output from a given set of inputs

Allocative Efficiency – When resources are used to produce the goods and services that consumers want and in such a way that consumer satisfaction (or utility or welfare) is maximised

Economic Efficiency – A situation in which both allocative efficiency and productive efficiency have been achieved; a situation in which society is producing the mixture of products that consumers desire at minimum cost

Pareto Optimum – When no reallocation of resources can make one individual better off without making some other individual worse off

3.1 MARKET FAILURE AND EXTERNALITIES

Market Failure – When the free market mechanism does not result in an optimal allocation of resources, thus causing allocative inefficiency e.g. where there is a divergence between marginal social benefit (MSB) and marginal social cost (MSC)

Marginal Analysis – A perspective to economic decision making based on examining the additional (marginal) benefits and costs of a change in activity

Marginal Social Benefit (MSB) – The additional benefit that society gains from consuming one more unit of a product

Marginal Social Cost (MSC) – The cost to society of producing one more unit of a product

Externality – A cost or benefit that is an external by-product of a market transaction, and is thus not reflected in the market price

Consumption Externality – An externality that impacts the consumption side of a market, and may be either positive or negative

Production Externality – An externality that impacts the production side of a market, and may be either positive or negative

Private Costs – Costs incurred by an economic agent as part of its production or other economic activities e.g. the costs incurred by a firm to produce a product

External Costs – Costs that are imposed on a third party due to an economic agent's production or other economic activities e.g. toxic fumes affecting local citizens, due to production in a nearby factory

Private Benefits – Benefits experienced by an economic agent as part of its production or other economic activities e.g. the utility (satisfaction) a consumer gains from consuming a product

External Benefits – Benefits accrued by a third party due to an economic agent's production or other economic activities e.g. someone getting a vaccine benefits those around them, as those around them are now less likely to catch the specific disease from them

Social Costs – Private Costs + External Costs

Social Benefits – Private Benefits + External Benefits

Negative Externality – This occurs when the social cost of an activity is greater than the private cost i.e. when there is an external cost

Positive Externality – This occurs when the social benefit of an activity is greater than the private benefit i.e. when there is an external benefit

3.2 OTHER CAUSES OF MARKET FAILURE

Private Good – A good that must be purchased to be consumed, and whose consumption by one person prevents another person from consuming it; such a good has excludability, is rivalrous (diminishable) and can be rejected e.g. a store owner can exclude you from buying a chocolate bar by not allowing you to have it if you aren't willing to pay a certain price for it. It is rivalrous (diminishable) in the sense that if you consume a chocolate bar, this affects the amount of the good (chocolate bars) available for others (if there was 10 units in the store, now there is only 9 units available for others, and now nobody else can consume that specific chocolate bar that you ate). It is rejectable in the sense that you can choose not to consume it

Public Good – A good that one person can consume without reducing its availability to other people, and from which no one can be excluded; such a good is non-exclusive, non-rivalrous (i.e. non-diminishable) and non-rejectable e.g. the government cannot exclude you from benefiting from the 'consumption' of national defence. Your consumption of national defence does not affect the consumption of others (if I build a house next to yours, we both equally benefit from national defence services). You cannot reject consumption of national defence because, effectively, just being in the country means you are consuming it

Non-Excludability – A situation existing where individual consumers cannot be excluded from consumption of a particular product

Non-Rivalrous – A situation existing where consumption by one individual does not affect the consumption of others

Non-Rejectability – A situation existing where individual consumers cannot reject consumption of a particular product

Pure Public Good – A good that has all of the characteristics of a public good

Quasi-Public Good – A good that has some, but not all, of the characteristics of a public good

Free Rider – Someone who directly benefits from the consumption of a public good, but who does not contribute towards its provision; when a person cannot be excluded from consuming a good, and thus has no incentive to pay for its provision

Merit Good – A good that brings unforeseen benefits to consumers, such that it is likely to be underconsumed in a free market; a good that has more private benefits than consumers actually realise e.g. education, health etc...

Demerit Good – A good that brings less benefit to consumers than they realise, such that it is likely to be overconsumed in a free market; a good whose consumption is more harmful than the consumer realises e.g. cigarettes, alcohol etc..

Information Failure – A lack of information resulting in economic agents making decisions that do not maximise welfare

Asymmetric Information – A situation in which some economic agents in a market have better information about market conditions than others; when information is unequally shared between two parties

Adverse Selection – A situation in which those who are at higher risk (more likely) of needing insurance, are more likely to take out insurance

Moral Hazard – A situation in which an individual who has taken out insurance is more likely to take higher risks; a lack of incentive to guard against risk where one is protected from its consequences

3.3 GOVERNMENT INTERVENTION AND GOVERNMENT FAILURE

Internalisation of Externalities – An attempt to deal with an externality by implementing an external cost or benefit into the price system

Government Failure – A situation where government intervention to correct a market failure creates inefficiency, does not maximise welfare and leads to a misallocation of scarce resources

Indirect Tax – A tax levied on spending on goods or services

Specific / Per Unit Tax – A tax of a fixed amount for each unit of a good or service sold e.g. £1 per kilogram of a product sold

Ad Valorem Tax – A tax levied on a good or service, set as a percentage of the selling price e.g. VAT (20% tax rate on products in the UK)

Incidence of a Tax – The way in which the burden of paying a sales tax is shared out between buyers and sellers

Excess Burden of a Sales Tax – The deadweight loss to society following the introduction of a sales tax

Subsidy – A sum of money given by the government to producers to encourage production of a good or service; a payment, usually from a governing body, to encourage production or consumption

Incidence of a Subsidy – The way in which the benefits of a subsidy are shared out between buyers and sellers

Excess Burden of a Subsidy – The deadweight loss to society following the granting of a subsidy

Regulation – The imposition of rules by government, backed by the use of penalties that are intended to change the behaviour of other economic agents to that which is socially optimal

Prohibition – An attempt to prevent the consumption of a demerit good by declaring it illegal

Minimum Wage – A system designed to protect the low paid by setting a minimum wage rate that employers are obliged to offer to workers

Tradeable Pollution Permits – Permits that allow their owners to pollute up to some given amount (decided by the government), and, if unused or only partially used, can also be sold to other polluters

4.1 THE FUNDAMENTALS OF MACROECONOMICS

Macroeconomics – The study of the interactions and interrelationships between economic variables in the aggregate (total) economy

4.2 ECONOMIC GROWTH

Gross Domestic Product (GDP) – The total monetary value of all finished goods and services produced in an economy over a specific time period; a measure of the total output, expenditure (spending) or income of an economy

Real GDP – The total monetary value of all finished goods and services produced in an economy over a specific time period, adjusted for changes in the price level (inflation)

Standard of Living – The degree of wealth, material goods, comfort and necessities available to a person or society

GDP Per Capita – The average level of GDP per person

GDP Per Capita Formula – $\dfrac{GDP}{Population}$

Circular Flow of Income – The movement of spending, income and output throughout the economy

Physical / Real Flows – A way of referring to the flow of factors of production from households to firms, as well as the flow of goods and services from firms to households

Monetary (Money) Flows – A way of referring to the flow of money from firms to households (in the form of factor incomes) and from households to firms (in the form of consumption payments / spending on goods and services)

Injections – Additions of extra spending into the circular flow of income

Leakages – Withdrawals of possible spending from the circular flow of income

Informal Economy – Economic activity that is not recorded or registered with the authorities in order to avoid paying tax, avoid complying with regulation (because the activity is illegal) or due to laziness

Short Run Economic Growth – An increase in real GDP

Long Run Economic Growth – An expansion of the productive capacity/potential of an economy

Productive Capacity / Potential – The maximum output that an economy can produce

Sustainable Economic Growth – Economic growth that can continue over time and does not endanger future generations' ability to expand productive capacity

Recession – Occurs when real GDP falls (i.e. when there is negative economic growth) for two or more consecutive quarters

Gross National Income (GNI) – GDP plus net income from abroad e.g. net income from abroad includes things such as property income, taxes on producers and imports, repatriated profits etc...

Gross National Product (GNP) – GDP plus the value of output produced by domestic residents from overseas investments, minus the value of output produced within the domestic economy by foreign investors

Purchasing Power Parity (PPP) – The exchange rate that equalises the purchasing power of two currencies by taking into account the differences in inflation and the cost of living between two countries

UK National Well-Being – Annual estimates of personal well-being in different areas of the UK. It is produced by the ONS (Office for National Statistics) through the use of surveys

4.3 INFLATION

Price Level – A measurement of current prices of goods and services produced in an economy at a specific time; the average price of goods and services produced in an economy at a specific time

Inflation – A sustained rise in the general price level

Purchasing Power of Money – The quantity a unit of currency can buy in terms of goods and services

Nominal Value – The value of an economic variable based on current prices, taking no account of changes in the price level through time

Real Value – The value of an economic variable, taking account of changes in the price level through time

Index Number – A number used for comparing the value of a variable in one time period with a base observation

Consumer Price Index (CPI) – A measure that examines changes in the weighted average of prices of a representative basket of consumer goods and services

Retail Price Index (RPI) – A measure of inflation that is used for adjusting pensions and other benefits, to take account of changes in inflation. It is frequently used in wage negotiations as well

Cost-Push Inflation – Inflation caused by an increase in firms' costs of production, arising on the supply side of the economy e.g. most firms use oil in some way, shape or form, and so if oil rose in price this would likely affect a large amount of firms' costs of production, resulting in them raising their prices to maintain their profit margins

Demand-Pull Inflation – Inflation caused by an increase in aggregate (total) demand e.g. If income tax falls, resulting in everyone, on average, having more disposable income, this will lead to a high increase in the demand for products in the economy as a whole. Firms may find that their stocks of products are running out way too fast, and so they are likely to raise their prices until people's spending on their products stabilises to a point at which their stocks are depleting at a steady rate. This can lead to an increase in the price level

Money Stock – The stock of money in the economy, made up of both cash and bank deposits

Real Interest Rate – The nominal interest rate minus the inflation rate

Inflationary Noise – The distortion of price signals caused by inflation

Shoe Leather Costs – Costs in terms of the extra time and effort involved in counteracting inflation

Fiscal Drag – People's income being dragged into higher tax brackets as a result of tax brackets not being adjusted in line with inflation

Menu Costs – The costs of changing prices due to inflation

Hyperinflation – An inflation rate of over 50% a month

Disinflation – When the rate at which the general price level rises slows down, but still remains positive e.g. 5% to 3%

Deflation – A situation in which the general price level is falling (i.e. negative inflation) e.g. –2%

4.4 UNEMPLOYMENT

Unemployment – Occurs when someone of working age is out of work and actively seeking work

Employment – Working age people who are either working for firms or other organisations, or are self-employed

Underemployment – Occurs when an individual is employed in a second-choice occupation, or is working part-time despite the fact that they would like to work full-time

Labour Force / Work Force / Working Population – The amount of people who are employed and unemployed, that is, those who are economically active

Economically Active – Working age people who are either employed or unemployed, and so are part of the labour force

Economically Inactive – Working age people who are neither employed, nor unemployed, and so are not part of the labour force e.g. discouraged workers, retired people, people (mostly women) looking after the home, working-age people in education (e.g. people in university), long-term sick or disabled etc...

Labour Force Participation Rate / Economic Activity Rate – The proportion of working age people who are economically active

Discouraged Workers – Working age people who would like a job but are not seeking one, as they believe that they would not be able to find one

Claimant Count – A measure of unemployment that is calculated by totalling the amount of people receiving unemployment-related benefits e.g. the number of people on job seeker's allowance (JSA)

International Labour Organisation (ILO) – A member organisation of the United Nations (UN) that collects statistics on labour market conditions and seeks to improve working conditions

Labour Force Survey (LFS) – A measure of unemployment based on a survey using the ILO definition of unemployment

Frictional Unemployment – Unemployment that occurs when someone is between jobs due to the inevitable time delays involved in job searching

Structural Unemployment – Unemployment that occurs as a result of changes in the pattern of economic activity. It is caused by geographical and/or occupational immobility

Geographical Immobility – Barriers to the movement of workers between areas

Occupational Immobility – Barriers to workers changing occupation

Cyclical Unemployment – Unemployment that arises during the slowdown or recession phases of the economic cycle

Demand-Deficient Unemployment – Unemployment that arises because of a deficiency of aggregate (total) demand in the economy, so there are simply not enough jobs available

Classical Unemployment – When real wages are stuck above equilibrium level, resulting in a surplus of labour supplied e.g. NMWs and/or trade unions can cause this

Seasonal Unemployment – Unemployment that occurs as a result of people working in industries that are not demanded all year round e.g. Santa Clauses being unemployed in the summer

Voluntary Unemployment – Unemployment that occurs when an individual chooses not to accept a job at the going wage rate

Involuntary Unemployment – Unemployment that occurs when an individual who would like to accept a job, at the going wage rate, is unable to find employment

Hysteresis – Unemployment causing unemployment

Long-Term Unemployment – Unemployment lasting for more than a year

Full Employment – Occurs when people who are economically active and also willing and able to work (at going wage rates) are able to find employment

5.1 AGGREGATE DEMAND

Aggregate Demand (AD) – The total demand for a country's finished goods and services at a given price level in a given time period

Aggregate Demand (AD) Formula – C + I + G + (X – M)

Real GDP = Real Output = Real Income = Real Expenditure

Wealth – A stock of assets that have financial value e.g. property, shares, bank deposits

Income – A flow of money earned over a period of time e.g. wages, salaries etc…

Consumer Confidence – How optimistic consumers are about future economic prospects

Transfer Payments – Money transferred from one individual, or group, to another, not in return for any goods or services e.g. state benefits

Disposable Income – Income after taxes on income have been deducted and state benefits have been added

Interest Rates – The charge for borrowing money and the amount paid for lending money (or saving)

Consumption Function – The functional relationship between consumption and disposable income; its position depends upon other non-income factors (i.e. wealth, interest rates etc...) that affect how much households spend on consumption

Corporation Tax – A tax on a firm's profits

Retained Profits – Profits kept by firms to finance investment or debt

Business Confidence – How optimistic firms are about future economic prospects

X – M = Net Exports (NX) = Net Trade = Trade Balance

Tariff – A tax on imports

Multiplier Effect – The process by which any change in a component of AD results in a greater final change in real GDP

Multiplier Ratio – The ratio of a change in equilibrium real output (the after effect) to the autonomous change that brought it about (the initial change)

Marginal Propensity to Consume (MPC) – The proportion of additional income that is spent on the consumption of goods and services

Marginal Propensity to Consume (MPC) Formula – $\dfrac{change\ in\ consumption}{change\ in\ income}$

Marginal Propensity to Save (MPS) – The proportion of additional income that is saved

Marginal Propensity to Save (MPS) Formula – $\dfrac{change\ in\ savings}{change\ in\ income}$

Marginal Propensity to Tax (MPT) – The proportion of additional income that is taxed

Marginal Propensity to Tax (MPT) Formula – $\dfrac{change\ in\ taxes}{change\ in\ income}$

Marginal Propensity to Import (MPI) – The proportion of additional income that is spent on imports

Marginal Propensity to Import (MPI) Formula – $\dfrac{change\ in\ imports}{change\ in\ income}$

Marginal Propensity to Withdraw (MPW) – The proportion of additional income that leaks (is withdrawn) from the circular flow of income

Marginal Propensity to Withdraw (MPW) Formula – $MPS + MPT + MPI$

Multiplier Formula(s) – $k = \dfrac{1}{MPW}$ or $k = \dfrac{1}{1-MPC}$

5.2 AGGREGATE SUPPLY

Aggregate Supply (AS) – The total amount that producers in an economy are willing and able to supply at a given price level in a given time period

Short Run – The time period when at least one factor of production, usually capital, is in fixed supply e.g. a firm does not have time to sell off its existing building, end a renting contract, extend an existing building or acquire a new building in the short run

Short Run Aggregate Supply (SRAS) – Shows the total level of production available in an economy at a given price level, assuming labour costs and other input prices to be fixed

Long Run – The time period when it is possible to alter all factors of production

Long Run Aggregate Supply (LRAS) – Shows the relationship between the total supply of products and the price level in the long run

Productivity – Output of a good or service, per factor of production, per period of time; the efficiency of a factor of production

Labour Productivity – Output per worker, per period of time

Human Capital – The stock of knowledge, skills and expertise that contribute to a worker's productivity

Capital Productivity – Output per unit of capital, per period of time

Depreciation – A gradual decrease in the value of the physical capital stock, over time, as it is subject to wear and tear

Net Investment – Gross (total) investment minus depreciation

Classical / Monetarist Economists – Economists who believed that the macroeconomy always adjusts back to the full employment level of output

Natural Rate of Output – Another term used by classical economists for describing the full employment level

Keynesian Economists – Economists who believed that the macroeconomy could settle at an equilibrium level that was lower than full employment / capacity

5.3 MACROECONOMIC EQUILIBRIUM

Macroeconomic Equilibrium – A state of economic activity where aggregate demand equals aggregate supply and real GDP is not changing

6.1 BALANCE OF PAYMENTS

Balance of Payments – A set of accounts showing the transactions carried out between residents of a country and the rest of the world; records money flows into and out of a country over a period of time

Current Account – An account identifying transactions in goods and services, primary income and secondary income (current transfers) between the residents of a country and the rest of the world

Visible Trade – Trade in goods

Invisible Trade – Trade in services

Trade in Goods – Export revenue from goods minus import expenditure on goods

Trade in Services – Export revenue from services minus import expenditure on services

Trade Balance – The sum of trade in goods and trade in services

Trade Surplus – The value of exports (export revenue) exceeding the value of imports (import expenditure) i.e. X-M is positive

Trade Deficit – The value of imports (import expenditure) exceeding the value of exports (export revenue) i.e. X-M is negative

Primary Income – Compensation of employees, investment income and other primary income coming in from abroad minus compensation of employees, investment income and other primary income going abroad

Investment Income – The interest payments, dividends and profits coming from abroad to domestic investors minus the interest payments, dividends and profits going abroad to foreign investors

Current Transfers (Secondary Income) – Transfer payments entering the country minus transfer payments leaving the country

Income Balance – The sum of primary income and secondary income (current transfers)

Financial Account – An account identifying transactions in the form of financial assets between the residents of a country and the rest of the world

Total Net Direct Investment – Inward foreign direct investment minus outward foreign direct investment

Net Portfolio Investment – The value of domestic financial assets bought by foreigners minus the value of foreign financial assets bought by domestic citizens

Transactions in Reserve Assets – Domestic currency, commodities (e.g. gold) or other financial capital bought by foreign countries minus foreign currencies, commodities or other financial capital bought by the domestic country

Capital Account – An account identifying transactions in the form of physical capital between the residents of a country and the rest of the world

Balance of Payments Imbalance – A deficit or surplus on any of the accounts contained in the balance of payments e.g. a current account deficit combined with a surplus on the financial account and capital account would be an imbalance

Protectionism – The protection of domestic industries from foreign competition e.g. this is done through trade barriers such as tariffs, quotas, subsidising exporters etc...

Quotas – Physical limits on the quantity of imports

International Competitiveness – The degree to which a country can, under free market conditions, meet the test of international markets, while simultaneously maintaining and expanding real income

Export-Led Growth – A strategy for achieving high and rapid economic growth through the stimulation of export activity

Expenditure-Switching Policies – Policies that increase the price of imports and/or reduce the price of exports in order to reduce the quantity demanded of imports and raise the quantity demanded of exports, to correct a current account deficit

Expenditure-Reducing Policies – Policies that reduce the overall level of national income in order to reduce the quantity demanded of imports and thus correct a current account deficit

6.2 EXCHANGE RATES

Exchange Rate – The price of a currency in terms of another currency

Freely Floating Exchange Rate – An exchange rate system whereby the price of one currency expressed in terms of another is determined by the market forces of demand and supply

Foreign Exchange (FOREX) Market – A market in which people are able to buy, sell, exchange and speculate on currencies

Appreciation – A rise in the exchange rate caused by the market forces of demand and supply in a freely floating exchange rate system

Depreciation – A fall in the exchange rate caused by the market forces of demand and supply in a freely floating exchange rate system

Hot Money – Money that is moved around the world from country to country in search of the best rate of return

6.3 INTERNATIONAL TRADE

International Trade – The exchange of goods and services across international boundaries

Globalisation – The processes that have resulted in ever-closer links between the world's economies; the process by which the world's economies have become increasingly integrated and interdependent

Multinational Companies (MNCs) – Firms that control production of goods or services in one or more countries other than their home country

Foreign Direct Investment (FDI) – The establishment of branches and productive processes abroad, or the purchase of foreign firms; investment made by an MNC in a country other than where its operations originate

World Trade Organisation (WTO) – A multilateral body that is responsible for overseeing the conduct of international trade

7.1 FISCAL POLICY

Fiscal Policy – The taxation and spending decisions of a government

Reflationary / Expansionary Policy – Policy measures designed to raise AD

Deflationary / Contractionary Policy – Policy measures designed to reduce AD

Discretionary Fiscal Policy – Deliberate changes in government spending and taxation designed to influence AD

Direct Tax – A tax which is levied on the income or profits of a person / firm e.g. income tax, corporation tax (called capital gains tax in the UK) etc...

Indirect Tax – A tax levied on spending on goods or services e.g. expenditure tax (VAT in the UK)

Progressive Tax – A tax that takes a larger percentage of income from high-income earners e.g. income tax (in the UK)

Regressive Tax – A tax that takes a larger percentage of income from low-income earners e.g. VAT

Proportional / Flat Tax – A tax that takes the same percentage of income from all income earners

Output Gap – The difference between an economy's actual real GDP and potential real GDP

Negative Output Gap – Actual Real GDP < Potential Real GDP

Positive Output Gap – Actual Real GDP > Potential Real GDP

Economic Cycle – The tendency for economic activity to fluctuate outside its trend growth rate, moving between high levels of economic activity (booms) and negative economic activity (recessions)

Trend Growth – The average rate of economic growth measured over a period of time (normally over the course of the economic cycle)

Automatic Stabilisers – Elements of fiscal policy that help to soften the impact of the economic cycle without corrective action from the government

Government Budget – An estimation of the value of forecasted government tax revenue minus forecasted government expenditure, over a specific time period (usually a year)

Fiscal Stance / Budget Position – The government's underlying position in applying fiscal policy, and the expected impact of future taxation and government spending on the economy

Budget Surplus – Tax Revenue > Government Expenditure

Balanced Budget – Tax Revenue = Government Expenditure

Budget Deficit – Tax Revenue < Government Expenditure

Cyclical Budget Position – The budget position in the short term. It is based on fluctuations in tax revenue and government expenditure, in accordance with the economic cycle and the operation of automatic stabilisers

Structural Budget Position – The budget position in the long term. It is the budget position that exists regardless of the stage of the economic cycle, due to the workings of discretionary fiscal policy

Current Government Expenditure – Government spending on wages, raw materials and diminishable goods e.g. teacher's pay, purchase of medicine for health services etc...

Capital Government Expenditure – Government spending on capital goods and physical assets e.g. roads, bridges, hospital buildings etc...

Current Budget Position – Tax revenue minus current government expenditure

Overall Budget Position – The current budget position minus outstanding debt interest payments

National / Government Debt – The total amount of money that a central government has borrowed, and still needs to pay back; the accumulation of budget deficits, resulting in the total stock of debt (plus debt interest payments)

Government Bond – A financial asset issued by the central government as a means of borrowing money

Fiscal Rules – Commitments by the government to limit the level of government borrowing to some amount over some period of time e.g. government borrowing can't go above 3% of GDP in a single year

7.2 MONETARY POLICY

Monetary Policy – The decisions made by the government (or central bank) in relation to monetary variables such as interest rates or the money supply

Central Bank – The entity responsible for overseeing the monetary system of a country (or group of countries) e.g. Bank of England (BoE), in the UK

Monetary Policy Committee (MPC) – A body within the Bank of England responsible for the management of monetary policy

Bank Rate – The interest rate that the Bank of England pays on reserve balances held by commercial banks

Quantitative Easing (QE) – When a central bank purchases financial assets, such as government bonds, in order to increase the money supply and lower market interest rates

Monetary Transmission Mechanism – The process by which monetary policy affects the inflation rate through the impact it has on other macroeconomic variables

Inflation Targeting – An approach to macroeconomic policy whereby the central bank is charged with meeting a target annual inflation rate that must be made known to the public

Symmetric Inflation Targeting – When deviations above and below the inflation target are given equal weight in the inflation target

Asymmetric Inflation Targeting – When deviations below the inflation target are seen to be less important than deviations above the inflation target

7.3 SUPPLY-SIDE POLICIES

Demand-Side Policies – Polices designed to impact AD through changes in government spending, taxes, interest rates or the quantity of the money supply

Supply-Side Policies – Polices designed to boost LRAS by increasing the quantity and/or quality of the factors of production, or by improving the efficiency of labour and product markets

Market-Based Policies – Policies that aim to allow markets to work more freely, and provide incentives for entrepreneurship and initiative

Interventionist Policies – Policies that tend to involve the government resolving what it believes to be market failures through increases in regulation and government spending

7.4 POLICY CONFLICTS

Policy Conflict – Occurs when two economic policy objectives cannot both be achieved at the same time, or at least not through the modification of AD alone in the short run; the better the performance in achieving one policy objective, the more difficult it is to achieve high performance in the other

Phillips Curve – An economic concept that shows that inflation and unemployment have an empirical inverse relationship, further suggesting that there is a trade-off between the two in an economy

Stagflation – When an economy experiences both high unemployment and high inflation at the same time

Page numbers in **bold** refer to **definitions**